# WE BOUGI

and turned it into paradise.

Written and photographed by

## Ceanne Harper

Published by
Perennial Publishing

First published in Great Britain 1999 by
Perennial Publishing
E-mail Ceanne@quarree.freeserve.co.uk

Distributed through
Constance Harper
Wenallt
Dolwen Road
Llysfaen
Colwyn Bay, LL29 8AZ

© Ceanne Harper

All rights reserved. No part of this publication may be reproduced in any form or by any means without the prior written permission of the publisher.

The right of Ceanne Harper to be identified as the author of the work has been asserted.

ISBN 0 9535704 0 1

Printed in Great Britain by

PRINTCENTRE WALES LIMITED
Mold, Flintshire CH7 1HA

Photographs by the author
© Ceanne Harper

Set in 12pt Times New Roman

The author was born in Manchester in 1930. Educated at Stand Grammar School for Girls, Whitefield, and Miss Wilkinson's Secretarial College for Young Gentlewomen, she began her career as a secretary for Holder Brothers Shipping Line.

In 1954 she an her new husband emigrated to Canada for a year's experience in the New World. Returning to the U.K. they settled down and raised three children. In 1962 the family settled in Mold, North Wales, where the author studied to be a teacher at Cartrefle. Five years later they re-emigrated to Canada where Ceanne joined the library service rising to the position of Audio Visual Librarian at the Chinguacousy Public Library, Bramalea. At the same time she studied for a degree in Sociology at York University.

January 13th 1978 saw her fighting back from an operation to remove a malignant mole. She had cancer. That same year she returned alone to Britain where she supported herself by establishing a new business, negotiating deals between television and young Canadian filmmakers.

She and Albert married in 1979 and continued to enlarge the business together. Cancer shadowed Ceanne. Treatment entailed more operations and a course of chemotherapy. Nevertheless, the derelict cottage conversion in 1987 was taken on with enthusiasm.

Enjoying many "senior moments" they continue to travel, work on the garden and live life to the full. Ceanne has started work on her next book, TWO WRINKLIES IN CHINA....

Thanks go to my Soil-Mate, Margaret Lynch, who suffered my gardening questions, shared her garden, and offered words of encouragement. Without her this book could not have been written.

Many things grow in a garden that are not sown there.

Spanish proverb

# WE BOUGHT A QUARRY
and turned it into paradise.

## CHAPTER ONE

The FOR SALE sign swung abjectly from a rusting hook. Anchored by a triangle of rotting wood its post rocked amongst wild undergrowth as a blustery November wind threatened to uproot it.

We stood in a companionable silence each wrapped in our own thoughts. My husband Albert, a retired Civil Engineer, was surveying the property with a professional eye. I, a photographer and dreamer, was willing my wish to come true.

Driving rain dripped monotonously from the hoods of our anoraks. We could taste the salt of the Irish Sea on our lips as the scudding clouds, urged on by a brisk south westerly, disgorged a wet curtain over the coastal hills of North Wales. The belly of the lowering sky pressed heavily as we peered at the dying house.

We felt an empathy with the derelict structure, its tears streaming down broken windows webbed in corners by spidery squatters. Fast arriving at life's terminus, we gazed nostalgically at a possible halt along the way.

The detached stone cottage had a forlorn air about it. I could feel a lump gather painfully in my throat as I reached for my husband's reassuring hand. He knew what I was thinking. I had 'terminal ' cancer which had shadowed me for nine years and I yearned for a large garden which I could paint with memories.

We had both been married before. Our partnership was already eight years old and we were searching for that 'special' place which would become a haven away from the fast track. Our early lives, so diverse, were behind us and we were embarking on a new chapter. We hoped to find a peaceful siding in which to enjoy our retirement.

Albert had never lost his love of machinery, starting in his youth with that magical Meccano set which he had traded in for his first motorcycle. Now he was preoccupied with vintage machines which filled all hours of his day.

'Can't believe how I had time to go to work!' he'd exclaimed soon after hanging up his slide rule. His eyes had misted with visions of days ahead spent with the smell of motor oil in his nostrils and the feel of machinery between his knees. He wanted a workshop where he could work undisturbed on the bodies of his mechanical mistresses - and, I suspected, to play with another Meccano set!

I, on the other hand, wanted a large lot which, like an empty canvas, would be the base on which I could interpret moments from life through my own palette of colours - nature's wonderfully varied flora.

As a photographer I also needed a darkroom where I could re-create on paper what I had captured with my camera. That was an essential room in a building which otherwise would just be a shelter to escape the vagaries of our British climate. Neither of us were materialists. Our needs could be counted on one hand - the machine workshop, photographic darkroom and, of course, the garden.

As we leaned over the crumbling limestone wall, to get a better view of the bungalow-cum-house, its pebble-dashed face stared sadly up at us. For some reason it had been built below the level of the road. In fact we had nearly missed it, stopping only when our attention had been caught by the insistent beckon of the creaking board.

The front elevation had two rectangular bays set like eyes on either side of a narrow front door. Its mouth of bubbled glass was draped inside with greying net drawn in at the waist. Rotting window frames were flaked with faded green and white paint, washed by yellowing runnels of fetid water escaping from broken gutters.

Behind glass, opaqued by grime, were antique green curtains, their satin fabric disintegrating with neglect. Like a black mandarin's hat the slate roof, slicked in the colours of a raven's wing by the incessant rain, swept down to the eaves.

As I reflected on its expanse, broken by two dormer windows which looked out sightlessly from its soul, my attention was drawn to a colourful parade of waddling geese. They clucked noisily around the corner of the house throwing inquisitive glances our way as they trundled past. Round button eyes stared unblinking as open beaks caught globules of water which dribbled down well oiled feathers.

My blood began to race. Excitement bubbled. Albert's hand tightened around mine as we exchanged questioning glances. Were they an omen?

'Welcome, welcome. Come in, come in,. It's your's. it's yours', their gravely voices seemed to call - at least to my mind. Not so to my down-to-earth Albert. To him they were just part of the ambient scenery.

Encouraged we stepped through the gap where a gate had once hung. Now it lay, broken and discarded, beneath a mat of brambles like a child's forgotten toy. Five crumbling steps, fragmented by age and neglect, led down to an uneven path. Rampant weeds, black and sluggish, clawed from cracks as mud oozed over a lichen covered surface.

To our left we could make out a dilapidated flat-roofed addition to the main building, partially hidden from view by a screen of ivy. It had a sectional glass door set so low that the water, which cascaded down the steps from the road, streamed in beneath the rotting frame.

The lean-to was roofed with a sheet of rusting corrugated iron. A mental picture of its use made me shudder with distaste. The scene was ghastly, enough to send any other prospective purchasers scrambling back from the brink of disaster.

Not us! We walked purposefully across the front, pausing long enough to squint through filthy windows into rooms which looked small and dark. Once past, we came to a row of palings, some hanging loosely where they had escaped from a twist of rusted wire. They screamed shrilly as the wind tore through an overhang of lilac which whipped leafless branches against the rotting spindles.

The path disappeared beneath a mudslide as it fell away steeply past the right hand side of the house. It followed the contour of the neighbours' half-finished stone wall.

Without warning the impression of a small, compact property dissolved as the vista unfolded into a wide arena. It opened out below us, like a gap in a curtain of clouds. The dormer suddenly became a three storey house, its basement hidden from view as it nestled snuggly into the rock face of a disused quarry. We gazed in disbelief at the startling transformation. Even the miserable weather managed to add magic to the scene as incessant rain dripped through a thick wall of ivy. I t stretched from the building to the end of the garden. Miniature waterfalls glistened over dark green foliage which ran for 80 feet or more. 30 feet high at the house it dwindled to 5 feet at the far corner where the quarry's rockface ran headlong into a crumbling stone wall.

That marked out the extent of the property line which stretched for a further 90 feet across the back, ending at an overgrown track.

My skin tingled with excitement as I took in the incredible scene. I had rubbed the magic lamp and my wish had come true. It was vast, a virgin field without any imprint of another's idea. I had found my canvas, my garden for planting memories of people and places which had coloured our lives.

Lost in a world of imagination I hadn't noticed Albert disappear from view. His voice, deep and resonant, called across the wind and thrashing rain bringing me back through Alice's looking-glass.

'You'll never believe it! Come and look at this!'

His imperious call came from dark recesses beneath the main house. Seized by the note of animation I followed his voice, negotiating a weed covered flight of stone steps past a dark cavern roofed with rough grass. It was doorless and my curiosity was aroused. I stopped, thoughts diverted by its eerie blackness. What on earth was it?

'Are you coming?' The words jerked me back. I stepped out of the dank hole, careful to leave cobwebs undisturbed. Feeling the urgency in Albert's voice I moved on quickly, making a mental note to explore the half-hidden grotto later.

'Come on!' The insistent note pulled, drawing me towards another dark entrance. Its large wooden door, devoid of paint, was propped up precariously by a sliver of wood. As I stepped over the worn threshhold an old familiar smell assailed me reminding me of my daughter in Canada. Together we had spent hours at the farm where her palomino horse and foal had been stabled. That same animal smell wafted through the series of rooms which lay dark and funereal beneath the main house. I half expected to hear a familiar whinney as I searched ahead into the darkness.

'They must be at least 12 feet high,' my husband declared, indicating the blackened beams above our heads, their shapes misted by swathes of dusty cobwebs. 'And look at the space!' His voice quivered with excitement, 'It goes all the way under the house!'

We began to explore, eyes adjusting quickly to the subdued light. Our sodden feet shuffled through the dust and rubble, stirring up clouds of greyish powder which irritated our throats. Slowly we moved through one large room into a smaller one lit only by a broken window high on the outer wall. It was like a prison. I shivered before turning back to follow Albert's shadowy figure as he disappeared into another room.

'Look here. There's an upper floor right in the corner. I'd have to build steps to get up to it, but what a great place to store wine.'

I grinned knowingly. That was something else which I had promised to do. Brew our own wine from the wild fruits of the garden. I'd already noticed several elder trees, as well as wild rose-hips and loads of brambles. Come Spring, there were bound to be plenty of dandelions. Already I could see the line of bottles, and smell the pungent scent of fermenting fruit.

'It's exactly what I was looking for!' Albert's voice broke in triumphantly.

'So's the garden', came my immediate response.

We hugged each other like children around a Christmas tree. Our gifts to each other were born of like-minds.

'Let's get down to the estate agents and ask for the key. We ought to look inside the house, although this basement has practically persuaded me!'

With a broad smile reaching his pale blue eyes, their life and colour enhanced by his spectacles, Albert gripped my hand lovingly as he pulled me back towards the doorway.

'It really doesn't matter how big, or small, the house is, does it?'

His question was really a statement. My own reply was as expected; 'No! You know my philosophy. A house is merely a refuge from the weather! The garden is what's important to me.'

I stared across the expanse again, thoughts crowding in as a burst of sunshine lit up the wilderness. Another omen?

'This is all I need. It's large enough to mirror our adventures. Can't you just see it. When the time comes to hand in our passports we'll be able to sit back and relive all those great times.' I remember adding, 'They've been special, haven't they?'

Cancer's shadow was still hovering but a light was dissipating its darkness. We were on the verge of buying a quarry, a challenge which would prove to be our private paradise.

# CHAPTER TWO

It took just three weeks of frenetic activity to negotiate terms and complete the purchase of what was to become a project of love.

The house was virtually derelict, being devoured by insidious dry rot like my own cancer. The quarter acre wedge shaped lot was dying beneath a thick knot of brambles, nettles and ivy. The prospect of its rebirth was daunting, but already our ideas were on the drawing board.

We worked out a 5 year plan. Stage 1 would begin with clearance of the land. At the same time a reputable builder would be brought in to gut the cottage and deal with the dry rot.

Stage 2 would involve us moving into the house on the heels of the builders. New fittings were needed in the upstairs bathroom, as well as in the re-built ground floor laundry-cum-darkroom and adjoining shower room.

A more appropriate fireplace was needed to replace an ultra-modern one which stood cracked and ugly in the lounge.

Those jobs were written into Albert's work schedule. Once completed I would then attack the decorating prior to us moving in.

Stage 3 was to include re-construction of an old garage which jutted out from the basement on the lower level. It was built of stone, and with some alterations would make an ideal base for an elevated conservatory.

Numerous flights of stone steps and associated paths were scheduled for Stage 4. In particular, access was needed up the scree slope which ran between garage and the quarry face.

These steps would lead from the garden, past the proposed conservatory and up to the back door. To their right would be a series of hanging gardens set into the rockface.

Finally a patio would be built outside the basement workshop. It would be sheltered by the garage's west facing wall and incorporate new flower beds as well as a narrow, raised dutch wall to take rockery plants.

The construction of an elevated wooden deck was noted under Stage 5. This area would be accessed from both the lounge on the second floor of the house, and the conservatory at its intermediate level. A flight of wooden steps would connect the two.

Stage 6 would see us moving to the far side of the house. Hidden beneath lilacs was a secret corner. Already we had found a shallow flight of stone steps leading down from the front.

The land there was steep, like the mudslide path, but with a little levelling we thought that we could create an intimate place set between more hanging gardens. The 'dark hole', noticed on our first visit, was earmarked for conversion into a potting shed.

Rejuvenation of the area at the front of the house was included in Stage 7. We had already purchased a large piece of scrub land which adjoined our property. The intention was to construct a drive backed by a new shrubbery which would screen the back door.

At that time we were unaware of a hurdle lurking in the future. My cancer was to reappear and cause a blip in our schedule. Fortunately the larger picture of our quarry project always took precedence leaving no time to worry about shadows in the future.

Reclaiming of both the building and land were planned to run in tandem. Work would alternate between cottage and garden. Albert would be in charge of all construction. I would labour for him as well as take care of the landscaping.

Each stroke of his engineer's pen pricked us with doubt as the list of jobs multiplied. Inner fears surfaced. Had we taken on too big a challenge? After all, neither of us were in our prime, and I, in particular, was well aware of running out of time.
'The best laid plans....', that old saying occasionally crossed my mind in those early days but Albert's vision kept me on track.

As the house plans progressed, so did the gardens. We sketched out several areas, some large, others small. Each was intended to reflect our travels around the world.

The property lent itself to this particular theme as there were numerous corners on different levels to give added interest.

Africa would be contrasted with China. Peru, India and Egypt would be captured in flowers, shrubs and rock. Even visiting wildlife would add special colour to the overall picture.

Islands of the Mediterranean, Canaries, Madeira and the Caribbean would all be painted onto my empty canvas. Each, when born, would stir up memories not just of places but of people who had touched and coloured our lives.

Without doubt, it would take a minimum of 5 years to complete the project. Designing, constructing and building up soil levels, along with raising appropriate plants to fit into the scheme, would be time consuming. Yet we were certain that each stage would bring with it a glimpse of the final picture.

The sale of our own house, some 40 miles away, was painfully slow. As a consequence we decided to purchase a second-hand caravan for use as a site office at the new property. Initially we needed a base from which to work on the outdoor plan. Later it would be used as a temporary home once the sale and subsequent move took place.

Storage space was a major problem. After much deliberation we added a summerhouse to the growing list of necessary large purchases. A small greenhouse would also be acquired so that I could prepare cuttings and seedlings ready for planting out the following and every succeeding Spring.

As weeks turned into months we sketched finer details onto the blueprints. What had appeared orderly in the first place began to take on the feeling of a runaway train. Perhaps had we realised what was ahead we might have halted in our tracks. As it happened, we were blinkered by the excitement of creating something which would make our efforts all worth while.

It was during that first month that we met a lady who was to prove invaluable when it came to the history of our cottage.

The day was unusually warm for early December and we had returned to explore the new acquisition. Our arrival appeared to pass unnoticed as we had approached by way of the rear entrance. It was reached off an unadopted dirt lane which also gave access to four other properties. We hadn't yet met our future neighbours but suspected that they would surface once we showed signs of activity.

Carefully we negotiated the narrow overgrown track, choked with dormant lilacs, and parked at its widest point. The house stood stark and petrified, broken windows on its back elevation adding to the sorry picture. Our courage began to ebb. Even the thin rays of a watery sun couldn't improve the benighted scene.

In silence we surveyed the site, each lost in thought. We both knew that it would take a lot of determination and hard work to achieve that final goal, and looking at it that day the project seemed impossible. A few days earlier we had brought some of the family, and one or two friends, to share in our good fortune. They had all been careful not to disparage our ideas, but hadn't found it easy to be as positive as we were. Furrows of disbelief had marked their faces leaving us in little doubt as to their views. To them we were mad. Perhaps we were. On the other hand.....

Across the discouraging expanse of brambles, tall couch grass and mounds of ivy, we could see the solid green wall which had been noted during our original visit. We had decided then that a first priority would be to denude the wall of rock which we suspected lay behind the glossy foliage. The word `quarry' had not yet entered our minds. Nor had the estate agent made mention of this unusual feature. His main thrust had been to get us to move on with the purchase.

Albert, a man unafraid of heights, set about stripping the rockface. I, on the other hand, turned my sights onto a long, dry stone wall which spanned the rear of the garden. It too was covered with knarled and knotted ivy.

We worked with purpose, each struggling to disentangle the invasive climber. At regular intervals we paused to evaluate progress and pass the odd comment. A small dent had appeared in what had seemed like an impregnable barrier. As

On our first visit Albert begins work on the quarry face. – The ivy hides a secret.

the morning wore on our spirits lifted. We felt that we were on the verge of discovering something quite unforseen.

'Hello! Is there anyone there?' The high pitched voice crackled across the silence. We froze, hands and clippers halted in action, as we wondered where the voice's owner was lurking.
'Hello. Yoo-hoo', it insisted. We moved across the open area, following the repeated call until we reached the bottom of the mud slope at the side of the house.

We both saw her at the same time. A tall, thin figure topped by wispy salt and pepper hair, stood imperiously on the upper level.
'I'm not coming down!' She barked, her rasping voice discordant against the image of a gentle, elderly dowager. She wore her high-collared, shapeless dress with great dignity, head erect, shoulders back.
'It's too steep for me! You'll have to come up here!' Her brows beetled above horn rimmed spectacles as she folded her arms across a flat chest.
'Who are you?' She didn't pause for breath. 'What are you doing here? This is private property you know!'

Feeling like naughty children we started up the incline towards her.
'We're the new owners,' I reassured her as I struggled to keep a foothold on the rough track, Albert's steadying hand in the small of my back.
'Really! No-one told me that it had been sold! My friend owns it but she's in a nursing home. I'm looking after the place for her. Got to keep vandals out you know.' Her rheumy eyes narrowed with suspicion. I tried hard to hide my amusement wondering how anyone could pretend to look after something which was so run down.

'How long has it been empty?' My husband's question was put quietly, its importance realised only by us. So far our enquiries on that score had been futile.

'Two, nearly three years.' Came the reply as our irascible visitor scrutinized us closely. She sniffed and frowned as she took in our old jeans and sweatshirts which we had thought suitable attire for the job in hand. Wrinkling her aquiline nose, she squinted hard at us.

'It used to be a quarry you know.' Her pale eyes misted with nostalgia.

'My friend's father built the house when he was a lad. Worked at the local quarry during the day.' She paused, straining to see what we had been doing with the ivy, then continued.

'At night, after work, he used to hack out blocks of stone from that quarry face.' Again she stared hard over our shoulders.

'You see those houses at the back?' Not waiting for an acknowledgement she rushed on, 'Well, he built them first,' She turned her gaze back to our crumbling house. 'then he began on this place. That was more than 90 years ago.'

I wondered for a minute if she was really that old.

'Of course I wasn't born then but my parents told me all about old Mr. Jones.' She drifted off into another world as she contemplated the wilderness below. Then her thin body stiffened.

'When are you moving in?' The abrupt question gave a lie to her expression which said, 'they're not moving in here if I can help it! They're probably squatters!'

'Oh, it'll be a while yet as there's a lot to do inside before we can make it habitable.' I hoped my reply would satisfy her.

She nodded knowingly. 'There was a bad flood you know. We had a dreadful frost last winter and the boiler burst. Nobody noticed it for a long time. It ran for most of the summer. In any case, we thought the water had been turned off.' Albert smiled back at her. `We did wonder. The carpets in the back rooms are sodden, all three layers of them.'

I saw the change come over her face. Albert was disarming when he smiled, and I could see her warming to him visibly.
`It'll be nice to have neighbours again.' she added, her rheumy eyes now concentrating on my husband. `You'll be able to do the odd job for me. I live with my brother. He's crippled with arthritis. Can't do much. I find it difficult to get anyone to come and change a plug, or even replace a light bulb when I need them.'

I stared at my feet, trying to control the smile which threatened to erupt into laughter. Her clipped speech matched the down-to-earth image. She reminded me so much of my grandmother who had lived alone for as long as I could remember. Their generation all seemed to be economical with words.

Our first visitor didn't stay long. Satisfied that we really were the new owners she retreated to her small semi across the road. She was to become a regular caller during the ensuing months, and a good friend who was missed when she died a few years later.

# CHAPTER THREE

That day her interruption gave us an excuse to take a break and examine the wall in more detail. The emerging face of fissured grey limestone cast its spell. Its exposed facade, shading from grey to pink and raw orange, was fractured and flawed and its unveiling revealed a myriad of fossils embedded in the rough surface.

The transformation was awesome. We stared wide-eyed at an enormous head carved naturally out of the rock by decades of rain, frost and sun. Like some ancient god it hung threateningly over the scree slope which flanked the house on the far side.

Adrenalin spurred us on. Excitement mounted as we set about uncovering further sections. It was like an addiction, we couldn't leave it alone. Niches and hidden crevices, all waiting like wombs to receive airborne seeds from rampant wallflowers and forget-me-nots, appeared as the curtain of ivy was torn away.

Without warning we came across an outsize fossil. Its discovery transported me back to Egypt, one of our favourite places. Over the years we had made several trips, not to unearth fossils but to explore decorated tombs. We'd even ventured as far as Abu Simbel on Sudan's border, and cruised on the Nubian Sea. Short excursions into the empty desert had rewarded us with sightings of ancient stone slabs etched with primitive drawings. Scattered across the sand these petroglyphs were not dissimilar to nature's own etchings embedded in our quarry wall.

The find was spectacular. It was a cross section of coral. 3 feet wide, it was shaped like a large fish flattened onto the rock face.  Above it was the glowering head.  Its skeletal frame on the fissured rock, puzzled us.  How could it be a maritime fossil when we were hundreds of feet above sea level? (In fact, from the second floor of the house you could see the hills which skirted Snowdonia.  The Irish Sea itself lay far below, completely hidden from view).

   Finding the fossil gave us something to think about.  It could make an interesting centrepiece to a rock garden planned to replace the scree slope.

   The metamorphosis had begun.  Our conversation played around ideas for the rockface which was slowly emerging with each snip of the clippers.  With renewed energy we tackled another stretch of wall before finishing for the day.

   Once away from the site we outlined ideas on paper.  The fossil was important.  Our subsequent research revealed that it was from the pre-Cambrian period of Earth's evolution about 570 million years ago, and we were right to place it as the central pivot of the rockery.

   I worked on plantings whilst Albert, the resident civil engineer, poured over the blueprint, devising suitable construction techniques for the hanging gardens so as to incorporate the fossil.  A sketchy picture began to take shape and our five year plan was duly conceived.  Excitement began to build.

   Winter creeping on decided us to make that first important purchase, the caravan.  We searched around on Costa del Caravan and found an old 28 foot static home ideal for our purpose.  It was battered, well worn and had obviously been in an accident, but it was cheap.  Arrangements were made for its despatch and placement on site so that Albert could convert it into self-contained accommodation.

As at every corner in life 'the unexpected always happens'! The day of delivery arrived. We had already voiced concern over the limited access from the back lane. We had been assured that there was nothing to worry about. A little man with long tape measure had been up and assessed the problem to his satisfaction.

'Delivery will be at 11 am,' he'd announced confidently as he'd pushed his bottle-top glasses back into place. It had crossed my mind that his eyesight might be suspect and had hoped that it wouldn't effect his reckoning.

We drove over early that day, making sure to arrive in good time. 11 o'clock came and went. Then 12 noon, but no mobile home! 1 o'clock saw us walking along the lane to find our new 'house on wheels' grounded on a rocky outcrop and leaning dangerously over a steep drop at the roadside. A four-wheel drive Land Rover was thrashing its tyres in loose shale as it struggled to push the massive metal body over the boulder strewn incline between bramble thickets.

Horrendous scraping sounds sent us scurrying back to the garden. Nervously we passed the time clearing and levelling the area where the 'van was to be sited - if it ever made it to its resting place.

It was growing dark when the monstrous brown and cream metal carcass, complete with dents and angry slashes along its sides, arrived at the end of the driveway. A major problem had been that the lane narrowed to a little under 10 ft at one point where hedges of beech and ivy encroached. Getting the 9ft wide 'van through the gap had proved to be a headache, to both men and mobile home. It's condition looked even worse than when we had bought it.

Still to be manhandled around a tight turn into our driveway we crossed out fingers and waited for the next act to begin.

The caravan-home is finally hoisted over the power lines, telephone wires and neighbour's greenhouse.

After several efforts, air thick with expletives, the heaving, sweating men accepted defeat.

'It's too long to make the turn,' they all agreed as they clambered into their jeep.

The light had gone, their decision made. Work was over for the day. The 'monstrosity' would be left in the lane. A crane would have to be brought in to hoist its elephantine body over the next obstacles - one neighbour's greenhouse, another's dry stone wall and barbeque, as well as overhead power cables! In the meantime, the symbol of our adventurous spirit would have to remain blocking the access road for at least two days.

We felt like gypsies, and no doubt appeared so to both sets of neighbours who had remained out of sight during the hazardous operation. We couldn't even apologise for the inconvenience caused and were fast becoming 'the neighbours from hell.'

D-day dawned. It was bright and sunny when we arrived ahead of schedule only to be met by an infuriated neighbour. He insisted categorically that the lifting couldn't take place with safety. The other neighbours were intrigued and stood quietly by as the giant crane was manoeuvred into place. Of course, it was possible that they were also concerned about safeguarding their greenhouse.

The job took a full day to complete. Commencement was delayed by the massive crane falling foul of the same boulders which had grounded the 'van. A heated discussion followed and that held up progress. Then it had to negotiate the narrow section before being met by our irate neighbour. His ensuing tirade stalled the operation still further.

At last, with sighs all round, the 'van was lifted, heaved and pushed into place. Once mounted on bricks we made a close inspection of the damage. It was minor and the small man promised to put it right the following day.

'Just needs a touch of paint,' was his assessment before making his get away.

By the time we were ready to leave for home we had been welcomed, if somewhat tentatively, by the neighbours whose greenhouse was still intact.

Happy with the day's success we returned to the blueprints which detailed tasks for the days, months and years ahead. A start was made on transporting tons of motorcycle bits and pieces from Albert's small workshop-cum-garage. He had adjusted jobs in order of priority. Now it was important that he get his `spares' into some sort of order in his new, larger storage space.

Boxes of screws, nails, engine parts, pistons, discarded prams, unnamed items collected from odd places over the years were piled onto our small trailer and towed across the miles to their new home. I had long before accepted that Albert was a `junk' addict and found it easy to go along with his phobia for collecting things. I had learned that everything always came in useful eventually, and so it was to be as we worked to create our paradise.

## CHAPTER FOUR

Whilst waiting for delivery of the 'van, we had uncovered what we thought was a small car inspection pit. It lay directly in front of where the `home' would be positioned.

On closer examination Albert decided that it would be ideal for conversion into a septic tank to take the waste from the caravan's toilet system. Its limestone floor was exactly the right medium for a `soak away'. With a few alterations it could be connected to the WC by a short length of pipe.

That was one problem solved. Appropriate action was noted in the schedule book to be referred to once work commenced.

The next was purchase of the summerhouse, our extra storage space. In the catalogue it looked simple to erect, but when it was finally delivered we found ourselves minus several hands to manoeuvre the heavy sections into place. It was put to one side whilst Albert concentrated on preparing for its location.

Reckoning on needing at least 1000 bricks to begin work on that, as well as other projects, we visited the local quarry. Little did I realise what an ordeal that would turn out to be. It was like going into the bowels of hell. The rough dirt road, beyond security fencing, was steep. Its unstable surface made it difficult to steer our small car which slipped and skittered across loose sand and gravel. Cautiously we drove on, creeping beneath huge cranes which hung vulture-like over the track. After negotiating several awkward bends, adrenalin pumping fiercely, we arrived at the office.

Our order was placed and delivery was promised for the following week. Then we made the return journey up the hazardous track. All the time I prayed that we wouldn't need to return to Hades ever again. I felt as ashen as the limestone dust which veiled everything, from car to machinery, to people.

The directional sign at the exit caught our attention. It indicated an overhead lorry wash. Without giving it a thought we drove our car beneath the row of powerful water jets, thinking that we might as well get a free wash. The fact that they were really meant for large wagons slipped past us. It wasn't until dreadful buffeting nearly washed us back down the track that we realised our mistake.

That same error was re-emphasized when we arrived back at the house. The car was still wet so I decided to wipe the bodywork down with a leather. That was my worst mistake. The car's shiny surface was no more. It was scratched as if with sandpaper and quite beyond repair. A valuable lesson had been learned the hard way. No more quarry trials driving for us.

The delivery turned up one morning whilst we were out. On our return we found the lane blocked by a mini-mountain of bricks. Fortunately the neighbours were at work so we were able to get on without battle lines being drawn.

Albert instructed me to move the load as quickly as possible. 'Use the wheelbarrow,' he was in his supervisory mode, 'and stack them in tidy rows behind the 'van whilst I set the mixer going.' With that he disappeared into the derelict garage muttering something about how lucky it was that he'd already picked up enough sand, cement and gravel to make a start. I watched Albert trundle our extravagant purchase of a bright red electric mixer across the wilderness. The opening

Anne tackles delivery of 1000 bricks, a back-breaking job.

ceremony, of years of cementing and concreting for Albert, was about to take place. A milestone had been reached on our long and strenuous journey.

So the erection of the summerhouse was moved up the list of priorities and work was underway. The base pillars, to take its floor, were soon in place.

A week later we were ready to raise the building. That was the tricky bit. The walls, complete with windows, were impossible for us to lift and hold steady. Our ageing muscles weren't up to it.

Luckily the builder's team of strapping young `demolition workers' were on site and they took pity on us two `old wrinklies' struggling in the back garden. I'd seen them grinning down at us as they'd watched from their precarious perch on top of the crumbling house wall.

What it is to be young... it took them less than an hour to erect and secure the 10 x 10 foot building which would store our meagre collection of furniture and clothes.

Whilst the demolition team continued to tear down the old extension to the house, Albert set about building steps to take a paved platform in front of the summerhouse doors. It was beginning to look like a pleasant resting place which could be used on hot summer days - if we ever had time to sit and relax.

The next acquisition was the 8 x 6 foot greenhouse. That building went up easily. Albert had laid a concrete base ready to take its light metal frame which he bolted into place. For the staging inside Albert had made use of some old office shelving. (I was reminded that all flotsam did indeed come in useful.) It was ideal for the purpose and cost nothing but time to make. Once in place I transferred seedlings which had been started off at home. They would be ready for planting out the following Spring when the soil had been over-wintered, broken down by frosts and purified. Another job was ticked off the daily work sheet.

Our home-cum-office, ready to be plumbed in, was connected to the power. With the phone installed, and contact made with the outside world, we were able to turn our minds to the daunting task of creating something worthwhile out of the horrendous jungle around us.

The caravan was positioned in a natural hollow on the quarry floor, its 9 foot wide bedroom end backed up to the flight of stone steps which we had used on our first visit. Along its length, at the rear, was a 5 foot rough stone wall which dimished to 1 foot at the bay window end. This soil retaining wall carried a broad path which bordered the party line. Our friendly neighbour was still working on a beautiful stone wall between our properties. When finished it would have a crenallated top which would add character to both gardens.

The van's kitchen window, door and small lounge window faced into the garden, whilst its large picture window looked south following the overgrown drive towards the lane.

The house and basement stretched between the 'van and the quarry face whilst the decrepit doorless garage, with rusted corrugated roof, made a natural angle for the proposed patio.

By this time I had thought of names for each section of newly planted garden starting with the one nearest the caravan. That would be the 'Garden Beyond a Window'. This idea wasn't new. It had already been used by the Emperors of China.

In Beijing's Summer Palace I had been intrigued by the variety of names. The Pavilion of Knowing the Spring, of Precious Clouds, of Listening to the Orioles, each was meant to explain its role in the Emperor's palace grounds. There had even been a Garden of Harmonious Interests, a name which particularly appealed to me. As my own plans evolved I found it fascinating to create names for each of my own new areas.

The ground plan was beginning to take shape. The scree slope, with its flight of steps and terraced rock gardens, would be named 'Steps of Life' and 'Garden for seeing the Fossil'. The elevated conservatory would be our 'Pavilion of Enjoying Gardens in the Rain'. I planned to fill it with exotic plants from around the world. The cantilevered balcony outside the lounge would be the 'Platform for Viewing the Garden of Memories'. It would be a focal point on the otherwise drab rear elevation of the house and would add colour through a series of hanging planters.

At the foot of the rockery a pebbled path would loop beneath a rough timber rose arch. On one side would be a terraced garden crouching beneath the rock face, and on the other, a rose bed raised above the lawn by a low stone wall.

Our septic tank was located half way along the quarry face. It was covered with a large, unsightly slab of concrete which we had hidden behind the greenhouse. Beyond that would be a large wildlife pond, my 'Garden for Talking to the Frogs'. (Years later I was known as The Frog Lady, because of my love for these strange creatures which I caught on camera, and immortalised in my darkroom.)


The pond would be separated from the greenhouse by a 6 foot high slatted wood fence. A lonicera nitida hedge would be planted on the water's far side to isolate this quiet corner of mini-Africa from the garden's work area.

Beyond the hedge would be an incinerator and compost each built of limestone brick to tone in with the surroundings. They would be enclosed by massive woodland trees, planted years ago in the neighbour's garden, and by the summerhouse.

The back stretch of garden, which contained the work area and summerhouse, would have two irregular shaped beds, one smaller than the other. They would be joined at their narrowest points by flowering shrubs and a small stone bird bath. That would be my `Garden for Enjoying the Butterflies.'

The final 25 foot across to the driveway was earmarked as a pebbled parking area between the `Garden Beyond the Window' and a narrow shrub bed against the back perimeter wall.

Because the living areas of the house were on the second floor views were restricted by the neighbours' semi-detached houses. Rendered in startling white stucco they tended to draw the eye away from the garden. This major drawback to our subsequent enjoyment of our `Garden of Memories' suggested a rapid solution. We would plant a row of fast growing cupressocyparis leylandiis which could be pruned into a 20 foot high hedge, a natural dark green backdrop to the gardens.

Because our property was lower than the neighbours at the rear it meant that the hedge would be much lower on their side, and it would be well away from their windows. As a consequence we didn't anticipate any problems.

That particular project was moved to the head of a growing list of tasks, and the butterfly-cum-bird garden was born. The hedge, on the garden's southern perimeter, would eventually become a bird nesting paradise as well as provide privacy for both us and the neighbours.

The plans looked excellent on paper and we were anxious to get on with the work. Only a late Spring, and poor weather, were to hold us up with the general planting.

The leylandii were bedded in, the summerhouse constructed. I laboured for Albert as he dug out the new septic tank for the caravan. As this civil engineer pickaxed his way through the quarry floor I stood by with the wheelbarrow ready to dispose of the tons of buried rock and treasure.

Throughout the short winter months we toiled in the caravan and the garden, working according to the perfidies of the weather. Our hope was to move onto site once the warmer weather arrived.

The 'Garden Beyond the Window' was outlined, all rock and debris removed leaving a virgin D-shaped bed ready to be planted. Two large half barrels, smelling deliciously of matured wine, were placed one each side of the van's ugly towbar. Lime weighted soil meant that a newly purchased red azalea and rhododendron had to be planted in their own private footings of peat based compost in order to survive. The barrels were perfect homes for these lime haters which would add a touch of colour to the empty flower bed, the 'Garden Beyond the Window.'

The caravan was operational and ready to receive us permanently once the old house sale was through. The summerhouse was packed to within an inch of its framework with our remnants of furniture and clothes. The basement had been cleared of rubble and a new concrete floor laid. Sodden carpets from the house, which we had found piled one upon another, were burned on a barren patch in the back garden. The smoke signals brought an onrush of curious neighbours, anxious to meet these strange new occupants.

At last we were ready to tackle the major project. Our enthusiasm could not be matched. As winter slipped beneath the fresh green skirt of spring we were ready to give birth to our `Garden of Memories', our quarry paradise.

# CHAPTER FIVE

It was Easter before we were able to move into our over-large cupboard on wheels. Glad to be on site we set about solving one or two problems which had arisen over the winter months. At the same time we were anxious to see some movement on the house renovations. Nothing much had happened since Christmas.

In January there had been a cold snap more like a return to the ice age. It had searched out a major snag, a burst water pipe in our front garden, and it wasn't our's. We were soon to be reminded of J. Howell's words of 1659:

>'A man of words and not deeds
>Is like a garden full of weeds.'

That heralded our first confrontation with the irate neighbour. In response to our enquiry he had informed us, none too politely, that their mains water pipe went directly under our house from the front road.

'That's where the stop-cock is, right next to your's.' No mention was made of the troublesome burst, which was why we had approached him in the first place.

I had looked questioningly at Albert wondering how he was going to deal with irate neighbour, and indeed if he had already come across this wayward pipe.

'Not only that,' the angry man continued, hissing through thin, tight lips, 'so does my neighbour's!' With each word his eyes narrowed and darkened. The effect was scary and disturbing. Triumphantly he pointed to the other white stucco semi, with garish red paintwork, which adjoined his property.

'They live down south. Seldom come up here. Nevertheless, they would't be at all pleased if you damaged their pipes.'

Such were the joys of living in the country. Already we had found that we had no mains sewerage, only a concrete cesspit. Now there was a problem with the water supplies, and with a neighbour. He had my attention not because of his rudeness, nor the fact that he towered pompously over my meagre 5 foot 2inches, but because I was concerned about the troublesome pipes.

Albert's slender 5 foot 9 inches matched his, but there all similarity ended. Muscles tightened in response to our neighbour's hostile body language. He was at least 20 years our junior with apparently little respect for age. Wondering what was coming next I continued to outstare him.
'And our septic tank is in your garden too!' His eyes anchored mine. I bristled.
'D'you mean that hole in our back garden?' We had already come across the crater covered by sheets of rusting corrugated iron screened by a dense mat of ivy. We had guessed its earlier use and had assumed, wrongly, that it was defunct.
'We had noticed it marked on our deeds, but the water pipes weren't!' I couldn't keep the coldness out of my voice. 'Where exactly do they go?'

The air crackled between us. He appeared to grow upwards and outwards as he drew in breath. Ignoring my question he plunged on.
'And we have right of way across your property if we want to take a short cut. And,' he added, his voice rising an octave, 'we have access to our garage across your drive!' He was airborn and flying! I had an overwhelming urge to prick his balloon. It's not often that I take a sudden dislike to someone but this was one of those occasions. Silently I dubbed him 'Unneighbour' for want of a better title.

Before I could react to his barb Albert iced my rising temper with a cool hand placed firmly on my arm.

'I had found a couple of pipes in the basement and planned to cut them off. Good job you warned me.' His voice was quiet and controlled. 'I'll concrete the floor around them.' Now, that got me thinking because I knew that he'd already done it.

Diplomacy is one of my husband's major strengths. On that occasion the touch paper had remained unlit, the situation partially defused by well chosen words. From his tone I knew that he had filed the conversation for discussion later. I guessed that he hadn't mentioned the problem pipes so as not to worry me further.

We didn't see 'Unneighbour' again for several months by which time the bad weather was coming to an end. On that particular day we arrived to find the front path flooded yet again. The repaired pipe hadn't lasted long. Water from their burst pipe under our front lawn was seeping through muddied grass, running round the side of the house, searching out cracks in the footings, before tumbling down the mudslide path. We suspected that the water had been gathering underground for some time.

Concerned at the possible damage to our foundations we drew Unneighbour's attention to the now urgent problem. Albert had traced the route of the pipes and found that they had originally been laid over the rock before our house had been built. They came out in the basement then ran under the house wall, along the side of the garage and across the garden to Unneighbour's property. It was a peculiar arrangement and extremely unsatisfactory from our point of view. We were anxious to get the problem sorted out.

It took three days for Unneighbour to come round and inspect the burst. Albert's usual good humour was wearing thin as he showed Unneighbour the damage. Anger bubbled when he found that even the law was against us. We were not allowed to turn off their mains water and had to live with the flood.

The plumber eventually arrived and, like a man who knew his job, surveyed the old lead pipe with dismay. It lay on solid rock just 2 feet beneath our garden.

'It needs replacing,' he announced, pulling an oily cap down over thinning hair.

'Yes.' Albert agree, 'we already knew that, but it's not our's.'

'It's had several bursts before.' Albert nodded patiently. The little man went on. 'It's really past its best. It's not deep enough either.'

I felt my stomach knot at the thought of them resiting new pipe under our house. Horrific images flashed across my mind leaving me despondent.

'Can it be taken around the outside of the house,' I tried to sound hopeful, 'or better still maybe it could be brought in along the back lane?'

'That would be expensive.' His reply was not unexpected. 'Perhaps your neighours would share the cost. For their own sakes it would make sense, and save them money in the long run.' I looked despairingly at Albert, not wanting to get embroiled with Unneighbour again.

He smiled confidently, 'I'll have a word with him. We can't risk having a flood beneath the house.'

That was one problem which wasn't solved satisfactorily. Unneighbour wouldn't go along with the suggestion, insisting that 'the pipe has been good enough for eighty years or so and should last a bit longer.'

Had we known at the time that he was planning to move away we would have pressed our case harder. As it was we resigned ourselves to the fact that we would have to remain alert over ensuing winters.

'Caveat emptor,' Albert had remarked philosophically, recalling Latin words from his university days. We knew then why our vendor's lawyer had been anxious to close the deal without the usual searches being made. In our anxiety not to lose the property we had agreed to wave that part of the purchasing procedure. That was another hard lesson learned.

The other set-back was the cesspit, or Unneighbour's so-called 'septic tank'. We had literally stumbled on it by accident. The pile of rotting corrugated iron, half hidden by undergrowth, had tripped me, cutting my foot and throwing me into a bed of nettles. Once stripped of its metal jacket we discovered the awesome secret. It was a deep, dark prison-like pit.

Left open as it was, it was a hazard in the middle of our garden. We were concerned that local children, who had been using the empty property as an adventure playground, might fall in and injure themselves. The danger was made more real because we were still not permanently based at the property. As a temporary measure we selected the least corroded sheets and covered the pit up as best we could. Our intention then had been to fill the hole in when we had time.

Later, after the altercation with Unneighbour, we re-assessed the problem. Unneighbour was approached and he agreed to repair it but, over the weeks that followed, nothing was done. So it was with relief that we welcomed moving-in day.

Once settled in the caravan we were reminded of the problem daily. The unsightly black hole yawned ominously in front of the new summerhouse. As a health hazard it proved to be even worse than the structural risk because the open cesspit was in constant use. It was an obvious invitation to unwanted rodents and several other nasties whose frequent visits pushed us to chase up Unneighbour, and his earlier promise. Finally, he informed us that friend of his had agreed to take a look and rebuild the pit if necessary.

It was a Saturday morning when the large, friendly man arrived gumboots in hand, business-like overalls draped casually over his shoulder.

We were deep into gardening with Alan Titchmarsh on Radio 2 and were loath to switch off but curiosity, about his array of tools, was too much. They were awesome. He had pickaxes, spades, hand chisels, ladders and what looked like dyno-rods. Quickly he set about opening up the pit even further than we had done originally. My pulse raced as his digging took him nearly to the base of the summerhouse. Visions of it disappearing into the growing hole gave me several unnerving moments.

The project held us spellbound as the internal workings of a Victorian cesspit began to emerge. It was still original, built after the fashion of the late 1800's. Effluent, from the houses at the back, entered through pipes at a higher level whilst the liquid drained away through, and round, a dry limestone wall which divided the pit into two sections.

The 'solids' were wriggling with tiny bright red worms, all working hard at decomposing the material. Strangely the smell was not as offensive as I had expected. Indeed it was quite sweet. I guessed that being enclosed, allowing the worms to work effectively, the acrid smell had been dissipated.

Once the humus had been dug out and piled to one side, complete with its army of worms, we could see how the original pit had been constructed. Standing on the lip we looked down into what reminded me of a family grave site. (I remembered to keep well away from Unneighbour. There was no point in putting temptation his way.) It was about 5 foot deep by 5 wide and 9 long. The whole area sloped towards our house. One third of the way along its base was a low dry-stone wall which stretched across two thirds of the pit. Set at right angles to the long wall it was in a dangerously unstable state. Several boulders had already fallen and rolled further into the gaping grave.

At the corner nearest our house was a deeper black abyss. It was about the size of a mini-car wheel and reminded me of the Roman communal toilet system which we had seen at Ephesus, in Turkey.

Once the `grave' had been washed out and cleared of debris it was possible to stand in the bottom and peer down the new hole. As our `cess-pit' builder worked at enlarging it, the darkness seemed to reach out to us. It was like the entrance to Hell. I shivered as I moved back from the lip. It would have been so easy to topple, fall and vanish forever.

At last the rods were assembled and the depth of the hole was measured with each piece. When they reached 22 feet it was decided that there was no point in going any further. Mr. Dyno-rod still hadn't come up against any solid material and assumed that all effluent must be washed away through the fissured limestone on which our homes had been built.
  'Wouldn't recommend pot-holing around here,' he commented drily as he set about rebuilding the pit. His humour helped to lighten the atmosphere which had stretched heavily between Unneighbour and ourselves.

It took a couple of days to complete the job, closing the enlarged pit with concrete cross beams. Finally, a metal inspection cover was set in place and we were ready to overlay the whole area with grass seed. We never anticipated having a picturebook lawn, the quarry floor's humps and bumps making that an impossibility. Now, with two raised mounds over the cesspits we were at a loss as to how to deal with the problem of levelling without trucking in tons of extra topsoil.  It was then that we decided to turn it into a `crazy croquet lawn'.  Our Canadian grandchildren were to hail it as a major attraction when they finally came to visit.

Strangely, the whole business of cleaning out and rerbuilding the cesspit removed any underlying hostility.  Laughter, along with plenty of ooh's and ah's had broken down a barrier which threatened to spoil the birth of our paradise.  That particular hurdle had been leapt and we were happy to move on.

The access problems were annoying but not insurmountable.  On the deeds it showed `access only to inspect the cesspit, and water cock', the latter being the one in the road at the front.  All we had to do was fence off the property with gates at front and rear which should discourage use of that ancient `right-of-way'.  Having been set up originally as a communal path, for the locals to collect water from a standpipe on the front road, its use in the 1990's was defunct.

The gates were especially necessary to contain Basil, our mischievous Jack Russell terrier.  He was a long term lodger, not really our's but as good as.  Unfortunately he didn't care for Unneighbour's Persian cats, so his restraint became a priority.  (The feeling was mutual as they didn't suffer dogs easily)  So installation of gates was moved up the list.

Once settled in our temporary home we quickly found out that you have to be both tidy, and even-tempered to live for any length of time in such confined quarters.  In actual fact, we found that the enforced periods of silence were both enjoyable and beneficial to our well-being.

I was able to move ahead with plans for further planting schemes whilst Albert spent most evenings cleaning up hardwood doors which he had recovered from the builders' skip.  His intention was to use them as garage doors when he got round to reconstruction work. Nothing went to waste. Door handles, screws and nails were all saved for re-cycling in due course.

Improving weather helped in our resettlement, plenty of sunshine re-charging our flagging batteries. It was nice to be able to live with the door open all day even when it was dull. The odd shower of heavy rain turned out to be sensually pleasant as it pattered rhythmically on the galvanized roof.

The van's metal shell soon soaked up the sun's heat giving a pleasant warmth inside - in the spring! Come summer it turned the 'van into an oven.

Basil had never been happier. He could dash about the garden, snuffle in the undergrowth and jump in and out of the 'van with ease. As luck would have it he also liked to escape down the lane and into the fields where grazing sheep tantalized his terrier instinct. The gates became more urgent.

When we measured the width of the driveway we discovered that only a large field gate would do. That meant stone pillars would have to be built to take the weight.

The next purchase was the gate. Fortunately we now lived in a farming community and soon located the exact item. Its transportation was a problem soon resolved. We took our small motorcycle trailer to collect it, tying the unwieldy grey metal frame across its back. Red rags at corners warned of its exceptional length and we were glad to arrive back without mishap.

With barely a moment's hesitation the mixer was wheeled into place and work began on foundations to take the pillars. Cement was mixed and laid, then covered overnight in case of rain. The plan was to start on the stonework early the following day.

It had to happen. The Unneighbour committee was waiting as we emerged from the 'van at first light.
'What are you planning on building?' The question superseded any welcoming 'good morning, nice day, how are you?'. Warm air was displaced by an icy blast.
'We're putting up our gate.' Albert replied quietly, his eyes unwavering.
'Well, you can't put it there. You'd better move it further down the drive.' M'lady Unneighbour was even chillier than her husband. She brought a cool response from me.

'Really! I understood that our land extended as far as the lane. We could have put the gate there. Instead we thoughtfully left room for access to your garage.'
'Well, it's not good enough. We need more room.'

Anger bubbled up as I looked directly at her. (She reminded me of one particular American politically- ambitious female.)
'And did you get permission to demolish the wall when you extended your house?' My fighting spirit had moved straight into top gear.
'That's got nothing to do with it. We want more room to manoeuvre our cars.'

My peace-loving husband intervened.
'That's no problem. We'll resite the pillar on your side. The gate can go at an angle.'
He turned his back on them, successfully closing the altercation, but I knew from his face that he was livid.

We waited for them to depart for the day before beginning again. By the time they had returned we had the pillars built, ready to take the gate. Our Maginot Line was in place, and a letter was in the post to our lawyer regarding the question of 'right-of-access'. We needed some ammunition if they insisted on continuing the border dispute.

As we continued to work around the garden the house renovations had come to a halt. Once the builders had demolised the extension, hacked off all the rotting plaster, and pumped lethal chemicals into the stone walls, they had vanished, leaving the evil-smelling cocktail to attack the wet and dry rot.

The remaining shell was held up by a forest of metal stanchions. The picture was depressing, the cottage more derelict than ever. It was difficult to imagine it ever being returned to anything like its former glory.

Nothing more was said about the gate. A truce had been called. Unneighbour's two cars continued to be parked in the lane, as had been the practice before our arrival. Their guns had been turned onto their other neighbours who had an ongoing complaint about access to the lane. Country living was proving to be less quiet than we had anticipated.

# CHAPTER SIX

Spring arrived, and with it came the builders. We awoke one morning to hear the sound of activity in the house. Throwing open the caravan door we were greeted by the foreman leaning out of one of the rotting windows on the upper level.

'We're ready to make a start.' he called out, his voice echoing around the empty quarry. 'The scaffolders will be here tomorrow and then we'll be able to take a closer look at the roof.'

With that he disappeared inside and the Ghetto-blaster was turned up to full volume.

At that time we didn't care. Excitement gripped as we realised that at last the real work was about to begin. Carpenters would measure up for replacement window frames and doors. The electrician would assess the extent of new wiring, an absolute necessity as the old power circuit had been a death trap. Labourers would tear out the cottage's heart and dispose of fungiied walls and rotting floors. A full transplant was about to get underway.

The winter months had flashed by. Albert had worked hard on the 'van, connecting up water and electricity. The telephone had been more of a problem but he'd managed it by trailing an extension from the house, along the side wall and across to the 'van. He'd even been able to connect our portable television to the old aerial on the cottage roof. Once the scaffolding was in place he would re-position all the cables in safety, the roof being over forty feet from the quarry floor.

To make more room inside we had torn out a simplistic table unit with wooden seats. Our own dining table, with folding leaves, fitted perfectly between the two cushioned bench seats which flanked the picture window. In emergencies they would convert into extra single beds   Removal of the bench table left a large enough area for Albert to install a shower.  That stood in a corner next to the enclosed toilet.  There was room, on its far side, for a small refrigerator with storage space for our twin-tub washing machine.  This arrangement completed the U-shaped kitchen area.

Opposite the shower was a sink unit with fitted cupboards.  Set at angles were more cupboards whilst an old gas cooker, between the two areas, had been replaced by a baby Belling which we had picked up second-hand through an ad in the local paper.

Beyond the kitchen was a bedroom which took a threequarter bed against one wall.  On the other were two fitted wardrobes with shelf space between.  Because we both enjoy books Albert built a double shelf unit on the window wall facing the bed.  Everything fitted in neatly.  The van's compactness left little to be done in the way of dusting - something which I had an aversion to.

The builders weren't our only visitors on that special day.  Later in the morning a pair of swallows swooped in from the south making several reconnoitring circles around the quarry.  Albert had opened his basement door to let the air in.  No sooner had he turned his back than the darting blue-black shapes jetted into the darkness, twittering loudly as they went.

We supposed that they must have been regular callers as they seemed to know their way around the old stables.  The position was ideal for nesting.  It faced south, and a small broken window high up above the garage roof acted as a safe exit when the door was closed.

Much as we would have enjoyed watching the nesting habits of these attractive migrants, we decided that once the basement was turned into a workshop it wouldn't be suitable for them.

That meant that we would have to dissuade them from nesting by boarding up their escape route - the window.

Nor were they the only ones to have used the basement for nesting. We were soon inundated with cheeky bluetits who refused to accept that no nesting was allowed. Each time the door was opened they darted in and squeezed themselves into holes in the stone wall where mortar had fallen out. `Pointing and whitewashing of basement walls' was added to Albert's expanding work schedule.

The noise from the house grew louder as work progressed. More internal walls were being demolished and further plaster chipped off prior to the staircase being moved to its new location. This unusual activity disturbed the peace and caused our friendly dowager to make an unscheduled visit. She had become a regular caller over the winter managing to overcome her dislike of the slippery path. Now, a few weeks of exceptionally dry weather had turned the mudslide into a rock hard track which enabled her to get down to the caravan.

We were busy digging out a temporary vegetable garden, behind the greenhouse, when she turned up.
`Yoo-hoo', her recognized call hit the quarry face and echoed around the garden.
`Are you there, lady?'
She had taken to calling me `lady' not long after we had moved into the caravan. I supposed it was because I'd managed to turn our temporary home into a mini-palace, making sure to use the delicate bone-china cups whenever she called for afternoon tea. I even managed to bake batches of scones in the miniature oven. These she particularly enjoyed as I tended to smother them with homemade jam and cream.

Privately we had dubbed her `The Dowager', but openly called her Nan at her own request.
`Hi there,' I greeted, automatically reverting to a Canadianism. 12 years of working as a librarian in Toronto

The cottage is gutted. Will it ever regain its original beauty?

caused me to lapse into my second language when caught off guard.

'Hi', I repeated, as I went to meet her at the bottom of the path. 'You're just in time for coffee, and you can try some of my new cookies.'

She held up a thin, wrinkled hand, diamonds sparkling on one finger.

'Don't stop for me. I only came to have a look at what you were doing with the garden.'

I found that hard to believe as she'd not missed a day whilst I'd been working at the front over the past week.

'I see the builders have turned up,' she commented.

Now, that's more like it, I mused, certain that her interest was really in the house renovations.

'Can't say I enjoy the loud music,' her voice brittle as she looked pointedly up at the open windows.

I grinned, somewhat sheepishly. I had to admit that the noise was a little over the top.

'Do have a coffee,' I encouraged. 'We were just about to take a break, weren't we?' Albert nodded as he joined us.

'That's right. In any case, we have one or two questions for you.' His warm smile enveloped her causing her eyes to light up with interest. She so enjoyed being looked upon as the local pundit.

Settling herself on an upright chair, which she had long established as her own personal throne, she looked straight at Albert.

'Well. What d'you want to know?' Then she glanced through the window and caught sight of the small cave which we had uncovered at one end of the quarry face.

'I see you've come across the air-raid shelter.'

'Air-raid shelter?' We both spoke at once, turning to re-look at the small crevice which went deep into the rock. It had been puzzling us for some time, but never in a million years would we have thought of it as an air-raid shelter.

'Yes. Old Mr. Jones blasted it out in 1941, just after the Germans bombed Manchester and Liverpool. The planes used to get lost and often dropped their load well off target. But, you'd be too young to remember that.'

I could barely suppress a giggle. Visions of people huddling in the cave were hard to believe.

'Actually, I remember the night they bombed Manchester.' My mind ran back over the years. 'I was about eleven at the time. We lived in a small village on the north side of the city.'

'Really? Where was that?' The dowager stared hard at me as I answered, 'Prestwich. Have you heard of it?'

She nodded, 'Lord Haw Haw came from there, didn't he?' then she turned to Albert,

'Can you remember the bombing too?'

'Yes. We lived at Whitefield. Not too far from Anne's, in fact. On the night of the blitz we were visiting a relative in Blackley. There weren't any buses or trains that night so we had to walk all the way home. I remember hearing the thud of bombs and seeing streaks from the ack-ack guns. The city was alight. It turned night into day.'

Nan drew our attention back to the cave.

'Well, now you can see why old Mr. Jones made the shelter.'

'Yes, but did the family manage to use it? And how did they all fit in?' My curiosity was aroused.

'He built wooden benches for them to sit on. There were only four or five of them at a time and, of course, the cave was larger then. It's been vandalised since by people helping themselves to the stone. It's in great demand now you know, especially by gardeners from down south.'

I nodded. That made sense.

As we nibbled on the biscuits Albert asked about the water pipe.

'Well now,' Nan began, settling herself more comfortably.

She loved to retrace her past, hardly ever having a lapse of memory.

'Originally the tap in the road was used by everyone in the village. It was known as the Communal Tap. In the olden days no-one had water laid on, nor did they have toilets or baths like today. In fact, most of the cottages were one up, one down, and were rented by the quarrymen.'

'So that place we found, at the bottom of those steps behind the 'van, was probably an outside toilet, was it?' Albert's mind had raced ahead. He was beginning to put names to places which we had found around the property.

'That's right. Once a week the night-soil cart came round to collect the buckets.'

My mind wandered, her words dissolving into the shadows. Night-soil collector. I had come across one of them in Xian, China, during a recent visit. I'd photographed him as he trundled his cart along a village street. Memories of that colourful visit came flooding back. With surprise I realised how far we had come in such a short time. Within the last century our own rural communities had been little different from those in China but now we had added 'en-suite' to our vocabulary. Even we were going to have two bathrooms in the cottage.

'Your house was the only one to have a bath after the war.'

The dowager's voice drew me back on a tide of memories to the present.

'We used to take it in turns to make use of it. Friday night was usually bath night.'

I grinned. It had been the same at our house when I was a child. I remembered the black-leaded kitchen grate being stoked up with coal on a Friday specially to get the water boiling. There was no such thing as an electric thermostat in those early days. Hot water had been a luxury.

'Can you tell me anything about the development of the village?' Albert asked, ever curious about architectural problems. 'I notice that there are several cottage conversions around which must originally have been single dwellings.'

'Yes, well, I suppose you won't know that in the old days if a man could build one room, with a fireplace and chimney, in one night then he could legally claim the land as his own. Of course, he had to have tell-tale smoke rising in the morning before he could be believed.'

'Yes. I think that was something to do with common land. I read about it when I was studying architecture but have never come across an actual example.' Albert was intrigued.

'Well, there are several in the village. Mind you, if you ask the people in the house at the back, not your immediate neighbours but the ones across the lane, they'll be able to show you the remains of one which was built before all your houses. Old Mrs. Williams lived there until she died about 10 years ago.'

That morning Nan had given us plenty to think about. Suddenly we realised that even in our own garden we might unearth some signs of the past. Already we'd come across several old mattresses buried around the garden, and we'd even dug up parts of an old motorcycle.

Once she had gone we returned to work with renewed energy. I was determined to plant out potatoes and runner beans to eke out our housekeeping and the growing season was well underway. Digging and clearing the bed was high on our list of priorities. Quickly we got into our stride. I used the spade whilst Albert wielded the pickaxe. Without warning I came up against something solid. Switching to the garden fork I tried to shift it, but without success. Albert was called over.

'It's a pickaxe job. Must be something large, like a treasure chest, maybe?' We both grinned. So far our finds had been valueless.

In double quick time Albert unearthed a large metal object. It was indescribably dirty. Black dried sludge clogged every crevice. Between us we lifted it and set it on one side so that we could examine it in closer detail. It was a puzzle. Albert scraped off most of the muck and suddenly, there it was. An ancient industrial mincer. Raised letters on the side announced Bollinger's of Stockholm. What a find. With a clean-up, some dark green paint, I would have an unusual planter.

Excitement at our find gave us new impetus to press on. Already we had come across a variety of bottles, some clear, some green and the rest brown. I'd even retrieved a couple of small stone jars which I'd mentally labelled `flower vases for the house'. It was as if we had discovered a rubbish tip and the collection grew as the day wore on.

By evening we had unearthed several pieces of old china, some chipped but others collectable. Among our finds were various household items. There was an old copper oil lamp without a base. Then there was a lamp base without its top.

Amongst the debris was a child's toy, a beautifully carved chest of drawers in slate made specifically for a doll's house. But the best find of the day was a heavy metal piece which, once cleaned up, turned out to be a brass fire-dog. It was just what we wanted to go with the fireplace - if we ever found one that was suitably ancient.

Altogether, when we'd put our tools away, we decided that it was work well done. The day had turned out to be one packed with information and tantalising items from the village's past. We were well satisfied.

The scaffolders turned up as arranged. It took a couple of days to build the meccanno-like structures, and then they left. They were closely followed by the roofers who checked on the state of the original slate, found it to be fairly good, needing only one or two secondhand replacements.

Inside the house the walls were down to the original irregular slabs of stone. They were huge at the corners and along the skirting but became smaller as they went up the walls.

The sight was horrific. In places, especially where a couple of old fireplaces had been taken out, there were massive holes in the masonry. Pouring through each gaping mouth was free-running, dusty rubble. These landslides rumbled messily onto wooden floorboards seeking out cracks and drifting through to Albert's motorcycle basement.
'It's called the infill,' advised our builder. Albert didn't say a word but let the 'authority' ramble on.
'When they originally built these stone cottages they had double walls. Rubble was put into the cavities, and that's what's leaking out.'
Like blood out of arteries, I mused as we followed him round. I hoped that that wasn't a different kind of omen.

The building was looking more derelict by the day. We found it harder to imagine it ever being made habitable, yet we continued to keep faith with our dream. Each visit saw us easing our way through stanchions, side-stepping structural hazards, and mind-drawing how it would look when it was finished.

'This'll be part of the lounge,' Albert mused, as he took in the area which once was a small corridor, cupboard and narrow staircase.
'Once the stairs are out that window will be turned into a doorway onto a deck outside.'
I dreamed on.
He led me through the forest of metal expanding poles which were holding the upper floor and roof in place.
'This'll be the dining-room. We'll have a new door at the far end which will lead into a small vestibule.' I looked at where the original long corridor had been. Now there were no walls at all. The frontdoor was still there but it opened into the complete groundfloor of the house, held together by stanchions,

At last the staircase is moved to its new location.

stanchions and more stanchions, and Albert's imagination.

'This'll be the hall,' he continued, as we moved around the open space, kicking up the dust.

'The stairs will be re-used. They'll go directly out of this room and up through the middle of the house.'
He pointed out where it would follow a right-angled bend in the wall.

We moved on.

'And this will be the kitchen. It'll be as large as each of the other rooms so you'll have plenty of space.'

When we finally closed the frontdoor the picture drawn was bright in my mind. Albert's vision was strong enough to carry both of us along with it and we slept well in our little caravan home that night.

## CHAPTER SEVEN

Once cleared of rubbish we attacked the back garden. Our efforts at burning the numerous sodden carpets from the house had left several patches of raw, scorched earth which would need special care before seeding.

As for the rest of the wilderness I was determined to transform it into a garden with a central grassy area which would be a foil for the flowers and shrubs. From experience in Canada, when I had worked on our two acre lot, I knew that continual cutting of rough field grass would eventually produce a hardwearing green carpet, not a 'lawn' but a useable area of mini-hillocks. So we got out the hover and began mowing.

Unneighbour watched our efforts over the wall. 'Can't see you ever getting grass to grow on that!'

His scepticism was aired each time the mower throbbed into life. Privately I wished that the leylandii would put a spurt on, and even stooped to feeding them surreptitiously with a miracle fertilizer along with gallons of water. Whispered prayers were offered up at regular intervals. Unneighbour would get a surprise in a couple of years when the two-fingered green tips would wave rudely above his wall. I could hardly wait. What a satisfying sight that would be.

In the meantime, we pushed on with the 'Garden Beyond the Window'. The rhododendron and azalea rewarded us by bursting into a blaze of hot colour beneath the picture window. A purple-leafed berberis, tucked in at one corner of the 'van, hardly grew at all, whereas, at the other corner a Masquerade rose, planted the previous autumn, was already scrambling over its trellis. I called it the Titchmarsh rose because it was born of a cutting set after one of Alan's Saturday morning radio shows. I was to owe that famous gardener a lot when the gardens finally reached maturity several years later.

Seedlings in the greenhouse were ready to be planted out. Pacific Giant delphiniums were already throwing out green shoots, as were tagetes, nemesia, and lavatera. I was determined to have annual colour to get us through July and August when early perennials would have thrown off their first-year floral gowns.

Waiting in the wings, ready to follow the annuals, would be autumn flowering asters, chrysanthemums and Michaelmas daisies, all still sparse specimens in their early childhood. Roses, retrieved from a friend's garden the previous November and re-sited in the 'Window' bed, were beginning to show signs of growth and were pruned back to knee height, (as per Mr. Titchmarsh's instructions). In June Superstar, with its strawberry scented vermilion heads, would blend easily with the lemon and pink frilled blooms of Peace. Nearby, red rimmed golden blooms of Sheila's Perfume would sit well with the dark velvety red of Ingrid Bergman.

In later years I found that all these hybrids needed a regular watering with Epsom Salts to help them survive and flower well in the lime-based soil. Chopped up banana skins around their feet also provided them with extra magnesium.

The delphiniums, shaded through purple to pale blue, were planted in the 'Window' bed alongside orange day lilies. Blood red peonies, transferred from our old garden, skirted patches of mauve, puce and lilac Michaelmas daisies. They were all part of my on-going planting scheme, scheduled to fill the garden with colour from Spring to late Autumn. A ceanothus was positioned to make a backdrop to the bed when viewing from inside the 'van. Its feathery brushes of misty blue crowning glossy dark evergreen foliage would share space with a white-buttoned spiraea. Once they reached maturity both would provide a shield of privacy for caravanning visitors.

When we had first battled with the garden we had exposed what looked like a dead tree trunk close to the 'Window' bed. Smothered in ivy its 5 feet tall bole, with several leafless sticks bristling from its severed head, was a problem. Not knowing what else to do we had stripped off the parasitical gown and uncovered a body tortured and twisted. We left it then, thinking that we might eventually train a clematis to scramble over its barren form.

As Spring moved in we were surprised to find the tree coming back to life. It was an ash, and gradually it stretched withered limbs towards the sun. A sparse canopy of pale green, delicate leaves fanned out from its skinny arms adding a touch of humour to the garden. It became a day centre for a variety of birds who visited a strategically placed nut feeder. It also made an ancient weather barometer, reminding me of a childhood rhyme:

> 'Oak before the ash, we'll have a splash, but
> Ash before the oak means a soak.'

Even Albert joined in the magic, planting out several oak saplings which he'd grown from acorns collected in the back lane. Their help would assure us of a reliable forecast to top that of the BBC's weather team.

We were glad to see the tree's recovery. It marked the edge of a newly laid, pebbled path, the curve of its trunk echoing a sweep made by a cushion of pink saxifrage beneath the Masquerade.

That corner of the garden was quickly brought to life by a regular parade of visiting blue, great and coal tits, along with rose-breasted and green finches. Even families of long-tailed tits chanced their luck in early Spring and late Autumn. Noisy twittering alerted us to their arrival. They were like children let out of school on a wet day, their tiny bodies covered with pink and buff feathers flitting like butterflies around the feeders.

Gradually our bird clientele expanded. Bull finches appeared amongst the thicket beyond the planned working corner. Flashes of rich blood red hinted at their presence as they hunted amongst wild flowers growing out of the pale grey quarry face.

Nut hatches, with stubby bodies and long beaks, often put in an appearance to show off their delicate blue and buff feathers. They soon learned how to cling to the mesh of the tit feeders.

Robins, blackbirds, magpies and collared doves took up residence as word got around that a new 5 star bird hotel had opened.

Blackthorn bushes, on top of the quarry face, attracted families of gold finches. These miniature birds, feathered in black, gold and red, helped themselves to the blanket of white flowers, which preceded the sloe fruits.

Each day brought a new visitor to the garden, prompting us to keep binoculars and bird-spotting books handy. The area was fast becoming a wildlife sanctuary.

The out-flow from our miniature shower inside the 'van proved to be a beacon to other species. Slugs and snails, emerging from the surrounding dry stone walls offered a succulent feast to our first amphibians and gardeners' friends, the frogs and toads. They must have been living in the damp undergrowth prior to our arrival.

We'd even come across a newt surviving in an old metal washtub brimful of rainwater. Thinking to help it survive we created a new home in an old shallow washing-up bowl. A large rock was set like an island in the middle of fresh water and the newt was moved in. Unfortunately, it didn't care for its new lodgings and vanished after about 15 minutes. It seemed to prefer the dirty water in the giant tub.

I had visions of all these creatures leaping about in the gentle cascade of water as we humans showered in the enclosed stall above. It must have been busy beneath the `van floor as these small garden friends made ready for their summer revels. I hoped that they'd keep enemies of my hostas at bay once I'd planted them alongside a stone birdbath central to the two back beds.

Unexpectedly, a larger visitor turned up, no doubt attracted by the generous helpings of slugs and other tidbits. Its arrival was heralded by Basil, our faithful watchdog, who soon picked up the alien scent.

We had taken to walking over to our local pub on warm evenings. It was only a 10 minutes from the house and made a pleasant outing along a narrow country lane.

On one particular night we arrived back to find Basil barking loudly from inside our cosy 'home'. As soon as we let him out he dashed under the `van yelping with excitement as he scrabbled about in the dust and rubble.

Albert fetched his flashlight and knelt down to peer into the darkness which had swallowed up a trembling terrier. Puzzled by all the fuss Albert searched carefully, his eyes following the strong beam. At last he picked up a familiar wagging tail. That was when he saw the dark, round ball - and Basil poking at it with his small paws. He was trying to turn it over, nosing it around in the dirt. His yelp grew more frenzied with each move in his doggy football game.

When we finally retrieved him, by his short tail, we found that his face was covered with tiny black mites. They were fleas picked up from our prospective, resident hedgehog. It took several hours of tender brushing, and a good shower, to return his milk chocolate and white coat to normal.

Hedgehog Harry, needless to say, was undeterred. To this day he remains king of his realm, living happily beneath the caravan, pestered only by neighbouring cats as Basil, our faithful friend and companion, has since died of old age.

Once word of our new garden spread around the village we were deluged with 'thinnings' from other gardeners. My reliable 'Soil-Mate' was in her element stripping her own beds to supply me with my first major plantings.

Soon we were inundated with masses of perennials but with nowhere to put them. Even heeling them into a corner was a problem. The rock floor made heavy going of our digging schedule. Paths were being completed before beds because of the over abundance of rock and rubble.

So the 'Garden Beyond the Window' was filled with drifts of pink heuchera, and aquilegia. The stands of red peonies were joined by a glorious double-white buddleia which was to fill the garden with butterflies in August.

Unneighbour managed to watch the transformation from a discreet distance, increasing the hours of his own professional gardener so as to match the progress of our own work. He wasn't to be upstaged, nor was he aware that his gardener became one of our regular plant suppliers, admirers and horticultural advisers.

The builders finally finished work in October, nearly a year after we had purchased the property. Gardening was over for a while. The greenhouse had worked well providing a supply of perennials many of which were already in place waiting for the coming Spring.

Aubrieta, alyssum and iberis seedlings, scheduled for the proposed hanging gardens, were growing on happily in trays. Pelargonium and geranium cuttings, along with fuchsias were resting in the greenhouse where I had installed a small paraffin heater in case of frost.

A special hour, dedicated to Alan Titchmarch, was set aside each Saturday morning. I refused to miss any of his gardening know-how chats which were full of useful suggestions. His advice was followed religiously. New ideas for propagation were important if I was to work within my budget.

Rose cuttings were set, as well as heel cuttings from a variety of shrubs. I had found an escallonia escaping over the rear wall. It belonged to our absent neighbour. Soon I had offspring sprouting in pots behind the greenhouse.

More friends offered their hebes, spiraeas, fuchsias and hydrangeas as transplant hosts. Come the following spring I would have a head start with the next planting phase of my blueprint.

Once word got out that I was a seed and cutting person I started getting visits from like-minded gardeners. One young fellow, who worked at the local crematorium, took to bringing me cast-offs from their memorial gardens. Any plants being consigned to the dustbin were rescued and dropped off so that I could take more cuttings. I was even offered carnations, mainly from funeral sprays at a local nursing home, so that I could take pipings ready for the following year. No gift was turned down.

The transformed wilderness was rapidly developing into a people's garden, named after many generous friends - Margaret's roses, Frank's buddleias, Tony's geraniums, Bob's hydrangeas and Soil-Mate's hebes.

Even people who we had met on our travels sent me unusual cuttings through the post. These added to my thematic collection. Eric and June's dodecahedron, an unusual evergreen shrub covered in yellow flowers throughout the summer, came as a special surprise after meeting them on a ship in the Baltic. The charming smile of this WW11 bomber pilot, with his delightful wife, will always be alive in our garden.

As the days drew shorter, so did the time for Albert to make use of the scaffolding. The roofers had long gone but the metal framework had been left in place for use by the builders.

Albert took advantage of their non-working hours to paint gutters, add soffits, and top coat all the woodwork. At the last minute he decided to even clean the chimney whilst the scaffolding was in place.

The job was scheduled for a Saturday, my own non-working day. Albert had planned his method of attack carefully. He'd decided to use a large lead ball wrapped in a cloth which in turn was tied round with rope. His idea was to drop it down the chimney flue from the roof.

I watched from the side path, heartbeats on hold, as he scrambled up the metal skeleton. At each level he manoeuvred planking into place ready for scaling higher. At last he arrived on a level with the chimney. The ground lay a frightening 40 feet below.

Slowly he let the makeshift tool nudge down the chimney, hoping to feel when it had reached the bottom of the shaft. Suddenly I heard him shout.

'It's stuck. I felt it reach the bottom but now I can't get it back.' With that he fastened the end of the rope to the TV aerial and began his perilous descent.

When we entered the house it was to find a pile of soot where the fireplace should have been, and the air was clouded with fine black particles. The chimney certainly had been swept, but now there was the problem of extricating the cloth covered ball.

After several futile attempts at playing the part of a Water Baby, Albert returned to the roof and began patiently tugging on the rope. Eventually he was rewarded, but not before the lead ball had escaped from its cloth cover. Shortly after I heard the thud I saw a small black cloud puff out of the chimney.

Unfortunately Albert was still peering down the hole at the time. Black-faced he grinned down at me.

'I think that's it.'

'Then let's call it a day,' I smiled back at him.

## CHAPTER EIGHT

Christmas was within sight. The builders, due to move out in November, were putting finishing touches to the rebuild. Outside work had been completed and the scaffolding had been removed. Only one or two jobs were left to be done inside.

Each day, after they had left, we checked where they were up to on the work schedule. The electrician had completed his rewiring. The upstairs bathroom had been plumbed in. Downstairs, the kitchen was waiting only for its units. Holes had been drilled in the new extension's brick wall ready to take a toilet, shower and washbasin. They were on Albert's work sheet of 'jobs-to-do'.

The interior was barely recognizable from its sad beginnings. Gone was the long narrow entrance hall. Gone were the four doors opening into separate rooms. Gone was the skimpy staircase which angled up past a long, thin window to a dark landing under the roof. In its place was the new door connecting with the yet-to-be erected deck. For safety's sake it had been screwed and batoned into place until ready for use.

The day when the builders had opened that wall to the outside had been fraught with anxiety. Solid stone walls had nearly defeated the lad who had been set the task of knocking through. Removing a couple of huge keystones, which were holding a section of wall together, he had suddenly vanished in a blast of dust as more infill escaped. White faced, he'd tried to hold back the landslide whilst the wall made ominous cracking noises.

Eventually he managed to hammer, push and drop one massive slab over the sill. It fell with a tremendous thud onto the ground 15 feet below. The house shook on its foundations.

Conscious of the possible danger of losing the wall altogether, work was halted until we could get in touch with the builder. His decision was crucial, and when he decided that the proposed door width be reduced, we went along with him. One battle with a keystone had been enough to persuade us.

'I'm afraid you'll have to lose some weight,' he quipped as he weighed up the problem. 'Even your friends will have to be cut down to size.'

Albert and I managed a half-chuckle. We understood his reasoning and for the sake of a few inches we weren't about to make a fuss. Blueprints can always be changed, as we were to find out once our own construction work began.

In the meantime the lounge, denuded of its unsuitable fireplace, looked barren and unwelcoming. Although we had planned to install a grate more in keeping with the age and style of the cottage we had not yet come across one. It was fast becoming a major headache as moving-in day loomed.

One evening, when carrying out our regular inspection, we found the young plasterer still at work. The subject of the fireplace came up.
'What sort are you looking for?' His interest sounded genuine.
Carefully we explained what we had in mind.
'We thought we'd like a Victorian, or Edwardian one, but they're too expensive. Can't say we like the replicas either,' Albert explained, his mind still toying with the problem.
'Would a slate one do?'
We stared wide-eyed at the youth, little older than our youngest child. Like a magician he'd whisked a possible answer out of his hat.

Without pausing with his work, he went on, 'I think I can get one for you from an old property in town. It's being demolished and the builders are throwing everything into the skip.'

At last he turned to us, 'Are you interested?'

Of course, we certainly were.

After checking its size, 4 feet high by 5 feet wide, Albert asked if we could go and see it?'

'I'll bring it around in my car.' Our young friend offered, 'would tomorrow night suit?'

We were careful not to show our scepticism. He only had a 'mini' and we couldn't see him fitting a large, heavy fireplace into it.

He read our minds.

'It's in pieces, and if you're really interested I reckon £60.00 would be a fair price.'

That settled it. If it suited us it would be well within our price range. Without hesitation we made arrangements to see him the next day.

At 6.30 pm his little red car turned into our driveway, its chassis barely missing the rock strewn surface. The weight of the slate preyed on its chassis which made terrible grinding noises with each bump in the track.

Then he started to extract the irregular pieces and place them against the side wall. Disappointment was rife as we gaped at the dirty white sections. There was no sign of the rich Welsh slate which we had anticipated.

His offering was an ugly duckling, its beauty hidden beneath layers of chipped, multi-coloured lacquers.

'It's been painted.' Again he was ahead of us. Carefully he began to scrape at a piece with his file.

'Several times, I would say!' He grinned.

His mood was infectious. We couldn't restrain our own smiles as we watched with fascination. Slowly the white gave way to blue, then yellow, then red until at last the grey-black of its slate began to show through.

We moved in closer, anxious to examine it. Our excitement was feverish. The young magician was exposing a work of art. Our search was over. Carefully we laid each heavy piece of the jigsaw on the ground, able at last to admire its ornate design. When it was finally assembled we stood back in awe. It was quite beautiful, needing only a bit of hard work to expose the fine craftsmanship.

That, of course, wasn't the end of it. We took delivery whilst still in the `van and spent many twilight hours scraping and chipping away at the thick coats of paint. The moment when it was completely uncovered was one of real satisfaction. We had achieved another goal.

Once stripped we knew that it was exactly what we had been looking for. All it lacked was a hearth. The original one had been smashed during removal from its previous home.

Always one to have bright ideas Albert came up with a suggestion. We'd visit one of the slate quarries above Ffestiniog. `We should be able to pick up a few squares which I could fit together into a hearth.'

Minds made up we waited for the weather to clear before setting off into the mountains. It was a perfect day. The sun was burning through canopies of red and gold. Snowdonia was being transformed as autumn closed in. We knew that it wouldn't be long before the first snow mantled the peaks.

When we reached the quarry we were taken into the sheds where several craftsmen were at work. Fascinated we watched as they held each slab of slate between their knees and deftly split it into slivers. The resulting thin strips were exactly right for our purpose.

For the sum of £6.00 we came away with enough pieces for the job. There was just one small problem, they needed to be re-cut to fit the outline of the fireplace.

Albert, not one to be defeated, built himself a bench with a clamp to hold the slate. In order to stop the piece from flaking he rigged up the garden hose so that he could run water over it. I watched in horror as he set about cutting it with his electric saw. Even Heath Robinson would have been aghast. The motor was waterproofed inside a plastic bag. As Albert cut the slate, water fountained in all directions drenching us, the slate, the bench and the saw. Sudden death by electrocution wasn't far from my mind. Someone was watching over Albert that day, and for many days to come.

Installing the fireplace was no easy job. It had to be worked out carefully as instructions had not come with the package. Albert decided to use bricks and clamps to hold each piece in place as he mounted them, one by one, onto a base slab of concrete.

The project was a grand 20 piece puzzle. To begin with, the chimney breast was only 5 inches deep. That meant that the fireplace couldn't be set into it. So Albert's first problem was how to anchor the monumental thing to the wall.

Its central section was of cast iron. Wired at the corners it was easily attached to the back wall using screws and non-retractable plugs. Both the opening and fireback were seated with non-combustible rope.

Then came the slate sections. Each had to be drilled so that screws could be inserted and metal straps attached. These were then screwed to the house wall. Once in place, every piece was

Albert checks out the final details after installing his slate fireplace.

backfilled with broken bricks and weak mortar which was then left to harden over night. I stood and watched with awe as Albert worked with dexterity. What a winner he was.

Finally, the heaviest slab had to be man-handled into place. I was hired as labourer again. The mantlepiece weighed nearly as much as the complete fireplace and it took two of us to lift it. That was after Albert had devised a way of fixing it securely. We didn't want any mishaps with visitors who might lean nonchalantly on it, thus pulling it from the wall – and perhaps vanishing into the basement below.

Metal brackets were used. One end was screwed into the slab whilst the other was sunk into the wall. More ballast and mortar filled the gap behind and made a bed for laying the last slate fillet in place.

The completed grate was magnificent. A wipe of linseed oil and meths, on a soft cloth, had heightened its rich colour and I decided to base my furnishing colour scheme around it.

Curtains of heavy black cotton, patterned with roses, birds and butterflies, Chinese style, were cut and hand-sewn over autumn evenings in the `van. To match I had standard and table lamps covered in similar material whilst the floor was carpeted in soft green.

The fireplace had focussed our ideas. Excitement filled the empty house. It was like a groom waiting for the bridal party to arrive. The 5 year plan was coasting along in top gear.

After that engineering feat Albert turned his energies onto installation of the kitchen units, closely followed by toilet and shower in the extra bathroom, and sink unit in the darkroom-cum-laundry-room. I trailed round after him, roller painting all ceilings and walls, leaving the gloss paintwork to Albert who was the true expert.

'Moving-in' day was brought forward as the barometric pressure suddenly plunged. Night storage heaters were switched on and we made ready for our first Christmas visitors. I began to practice my musical presentation on our electronic organ. It wouldn't be a soiree but a coffee and carol singing party for the neighbours. (My idea of showing a white flag!)

Work on the garden was put on hold until April. We felt that we had earned our planned adventure to Peru which would get us through February and into March.

All thought of cancer was pushed to the back of my mind. I felt really well and took advantage of the calm to achieve another ambition - to visit Lake Titicaca, cross the Andes by train, and explore the ruins of Machu Picchu. I hoped to collect more memories there to include in the overall garden plan.

## CHAPTER NINE

We weren't exactly refreshed after our jaunt to Peru. I had succumbed to sunstroke, dysentry and high altitude sickness. We had been waylaid by pickpockets, held at gun-point by corrupt policemen, and felt ourselves lucky to have escaped with our lives.

Even the Foreign Office had warned about the activities of the Shining Path Guerillas.

'British subjects must be aware of the dangers in Peru, especially when travelling by train to Machu Picchu.' The cryptic official message had flicked at our courage throughout hazardous journeys by coach, train and plane across desert and mountains. We were indeed lucky to get back in one piece.

It took a few weeks for us to recover our equilibrium. The trip had been exciting. Or so we had decided, once back in the safety of our home. Slides, photographs and jottings of the adventure had been filed and we were ready to return to `work'.

Dust was blown off the blueprints. The list of jobs, which seemed never-ending, was pinned back on the wall. Scheduled next was the rebuilding of our old garage, a precurser to construction of the conservatory.

Albert, the Civil Engineer, donned his metaphorical tin hat. Under instruction, I unearthed my labourer's overalls and waited in the wings my mind playing with thoughts of Peru's ancient Incan Civilisation. I had been fascinated by their use of terraces to contain soil for planting, a construction technique which would suit several corners of our own garden.

In particular, there was the problematic area above the defunct 'loo house', soon to become a potting shed. The existing bed, on that upper level, sloped steeply from the front path to steps alongside the 'loo'. What was left of the soil was hard and unworkable, weeds and weather having seen to that. Terracing was the obvious answer. I made a mental note to add it to the list.

The building itself would have to be demolished and rebuilt using our own quarry stone. An interested neighbour had already donated a load of cast-off undersized slates known as 'Ladies'. They were ringed for Albert's roofing projects, of which the potting shed was one. The other would be the reconstructed garage.

Meanwhile, as I waited for further instructions, I pickaxed holes in that sunny corner. As I filled them with a home-made peat based compost, ready to make a temporary bed for strawberry plants, I thought more seriously about the long-delayed construction of a compost and incinerator. If I was going to improve soil quality around the garden it was essential that the compost, at least, was set in motion.

As soon as the last strawberry plant had been knuckled into place I thought ahead to the expected crop of delicious fruit. In anticipation of a good harvest the following summer I set about collecting jam pots to act as mini-greenhouses, a deterrant for birds and slugs. I knew that blackbirds were especially partial to a strawberry feast without the cream.

'It'll mean getting the concrete mixer going yet again.' Albert's words greeted me a few days after I'd settled the last plant in place. I was about to start on the vegetable patch when his call to arms came.

As on several occasions my own plans had to be put on hold. Emptying cold frames, made from old house windows, and pricking out greenhouse seedlings would also have to wait. Construction work again headed our daily work sheet. That always took precedence over greenhouse jobs.

'To begin with I'll have to rebuild the old stone walls. There's too much of a slope to them and they need strengthening to take the floor joists.' Albert often talked aloud to himself and this day was no different. As he spoke he set about pulling down a wall which had been erected some eighty years before, its huge slabs of limestone still fixed firmly together.
'Not quite like those Incan walls in Cuzco,' he remarked as dust and slivers of stone flew into the air with each thrust of his chisel.

Like our old house, the wall had been constructed by a craftsman, but unlike the Incas he had used mortar as an adhesive rather than cutting each piece to match its neighbour. The fit of stones wasn't bad, but the crumbling filler made the wall's demolition dangerous. As a consequence it took longer than anticipated especially when we came across yet another burst water pipe.

It lay directly underneath the side wall of the garage and breaching of the pipe was unavoidable. As soon as we realised what had happened Albert went round to Unneighbour's to give him the news. This time he came straight round. He had to because we'd turned off both mains supplies not knowing which house the burst actually belonged to.

'You're lucky there,' Unneighbour was unperturbed. 'It's not our's, and the Jones' will be away until next summer. So I suggest you leave their water off but turn our's back on.'
'O.K. but what about the burst pipe?'
'You'll need to call them and find out what they want you to do.' With that Unneighbour departed, returning only to give us a contact telephone number.

'The problem's all your's. I wish you luck,' were his parting words. Unexpectedly for Unneighbour, his wishes proved all-powerful. An urgent phone call ended up with Albert mentioning the troublesome pipes beneath our house. The result was that arrangements were made for new conduits to be brought in along the back lane directly into their pair of semis. All costs were shared by them, and we got a satisfactory result without too much hassle.

It wasn't until a series of prospective buyers began to roll up at Unneighbour's property that we realised why he'd had such an out-of-character a change of heart. Then we got drawn into new discussions about the 'right of access' as well as the demarkation of our property.

It all came to a head one day when I was hanging out the washing. Loud voices behind Albert's newly erected fence drew my attention. From the parking area I was out of sight yet couldn't avoid eavesdropping.

Unneighbour was busy explaining that there was a short cut to the village across our garden. Blood rushed to my face as I realised what he was suggesting. Even though the water pipes had been moved he was still banking on the old clause about access being applicable. Before I could speak out, and let them know I was within earshot, he went on,
 'And, if you have trouble backing out of the garage you can open their gate and use the drive.'
 'And what about those trees?' the bodiless voice went on.
 'Which ones?'
 'The leylandii. You can just see them sprouting over the wall. I don't want to have to look at them from the windows. I'd rather see their garden.'
 'Well, you could buy a piece of land. There's certainly too much for one house, and your septic tank would then be on your own property.'

The cheek of it. I felt my anger begin to surface.

'The land's not for sale.' My words were intentionally loud as I walked to the gate where Unneighbour and his prospective buyer were standing.

'But you don't need all that space,' the woman persisted.

'I'm afraid we do. That was why we bought the property in the first place. Good-day.'

There were no more altercations. Unneighbour turned the house sale over to professionals and eventually we welcomed new owners who were happy with the property as it was. They even helped us to install another gate to replace the original wall which Unneighbour had knocked down. That meant that our drive was enclosed once more, yet New Neighbours still had limited access, purely to reach their garage.

We were well into summer before Albert was ready to raise the roof joists of the rejuvenated garage. The blast of war from Unneighbour was soon forgotten as we settled down to complete the work which had been interrupted by both the burst, and the altercation.

Fortunately the weather was good that year. We'd had hardly any rain so work progressed steadily. The walls were rebuilt, and a new lintel set in place over the doorway. Albert even managed to incorporate a small window to one side of the opening which would eventually take double doors. They had been in his mind when he'd rescued the pine ones early on in the house rebuild. When bolted together in pairs they turned into two extra wide garage doors. The eventual opening gave ideal access for storage of a variety of items one of which included our vintage three-wheeler, named Katie.

This particular machine had drawn the Dowager's attention not long after we had moved in. On one of her regular tours of inspection she had spied it hidden beneath an old sheet.

74

'What've you got there?' Always the lady she hadn't attempted to uncover Albert's prize possession.

'It's an old Morgan,' he'd replied, drawing the oily sheet slowly off the flaming red body of his racing machine.

'Ooohh...' Her gasp told us everything. She was impressed.

'That's really old, isn't it? I remember father talking about them years ago. The manager at the quarry had one. Before the war, I think it was.'

'That's about right,' Albert concurred, 'she was built in 1932.'

Nan was intrigued. 'Did it belong to your father?'

'Oh no, Anne and I bought her a few years ago. We had had a couple of accidents on the 'bike and she'd lost her nerve. Riding pillion became taboo, so I thought this would suit her better.'

As they spoke my mind drifted back to those early days with Katie, our rowdy eye-catching machine. We had done a lot of travelling in her, breaking down frequently and always in out-of-the-way places.

One year we had driven 1700 miles around the Highlands of Scotland. On the way back to North Wales we'd taken a detour so as to attend a rally in Northumberland. By a stroke of ill luck we only managed to get as far as the Borders before clunking to an unscheduled halt. One of the valves had burned out and even Albert's expertise with motorcycle engines wasn't sufficient to help us on our way. To top it all it was coming up to annual holidays in the industrial northeast.

Fortunately we came to a halt outside an ancient roadhouse which meant that at least we had somewhere to stay whilst urgent repairs were made. Albert, with help from the friendly landlord, located an even more friendly works manager who set 'one of his lads' on the job. It was a favour, done gladly and with interest. The quality of the work was excellent and the final bill minimal. That said a great deal about the helpful people of that little-known corner of the U.K.

I remembered too how I'd had to sit down gingerly for at least three months after that particular expedition. The Morgan's lack of springing had put a dent in the tail of my spine, and at nearly 60 my bones weren't getting any younger.

We'd also toured Southern Ireland, a country where there were more pot-holes than tarmac. The rain too, locally called `a gentle mist', had drenched us on many occasions due to dear Katie's lack of a roof. We always took a golf umbrella with us in case we got caught in a downpour. Never-the-less, they were fun days even though we'd spent many hours sitting at the side of the road under the huge multi-coloured canopy.

`So that's why you bought the house is it?' Nan's voice had pulled me back to the present. `I suppose you needed somewhere to garage this little beauty.'

I couldn't help smiling. Our flaming Katie had cast a spell over the Dowager just as she had over us so many years before.

On all subsequent visits Nan made a point of asking after `the beauty' when she called round. Albert even promised to give her a ride once the days warmed up and our work schedule was complete. Unfortunately, our good friend died before he could keep his promise.

Work on the garage continued apace without too many problems. I was dismissed once the joists had been lifted. Whilst Albert hammered down the sheets of thick waferboard, cut specially to size by the supplier and which would take the conservatory, I retired to the greenhouse where my own garden blueprints dictated the next stages of husbandry.

The hanging gardens were still just ideas on paper. They would be moved up my schedule once Albert had built the new steps to the conservatory. In the meantime, I worked on embellishing the back border.

Work progresses. Albert tackles the groundwork necessary for installation of the new garage roof-cum-conservatory floor.

Original scouring of the quarry floor, removing tons of rock, had left only a minimal layer of topsoil. It became obvious that, before I could plant, I would have to improve its quality by incorporating tons of peat along with Fish, Bone and Blood. So I set about producing more self-made loam ready for use in the two beds which lay, like butterflies' wings, against the line of leylandii.

They were coming along nicely in front of Unneighbour's wall but looked rather sparse in their infancy. So I planned to front them with a variety of buddleias, senecio, hebe, spirea and berberis.

One particular shrub, the Darwinii, with its delicate orange rosettes had appealed to me when I'd ploughed through my gardener's bible, the R.H.S's Dictionary of Plants. Unfortunately, it later became a bane in Albert's life each time he got the mower out. Its prickles always seemed to reach in his direction, never in mine. Eventually it was to die away under Albert's constant tongue lashing.

The previous autumn's transplants of roses were doing well in their bed beside the summerhouse. A reddish-purple buddleia and Trevor's yellow flowering kerria made a backdrop behind them whilst another buddleia, a globus, umbrellaed the corner with yellow pompoms in early Spring.

A bright red and yellow unscented honeysuckle, planted at the corner of the summerhouse soon after it was erected, had started its scramble up the side wall. Eventually it too fanned out over the rose bed.

The Darwinii was planted about one third along that rear bed, next to a lilac hebe and a senecio which had been donated by another friend. That particular yellow flowered shrub had been mature when it had been offered. Transportation in our

Albert commences work laying slates on the garage roof.

small Datsun caused great amusement. It sat spread eagled on the backseat, wrinkled arms scratching at my neck like a mischievous pensioner.

At the corner nearest the drive was a bridal wreath spirea, and as an after-thought, I married it to a delicate lemon cytisus which crinolined at its feet.

As I continued with my digging, soil improvement and planting, Albert reached a delicate stage of his reconstruction work. The garage was to have a new slate roof, an overhanging extension of the conservatory floor. That meant that it would be both long, steep and shallow, an unusual and difficult combination. It turned out to be a challenging experience as Albert hadn't attempted roofing before.

Delving into his large library of D.I.Y. books he found one which detailed procedures. Following instructions he began by covering the rafters with a heavy gauge polythene. He had looked into the cost of using roofing felt and decided that it would be an unnecessary expense on a garage.

Next he nailed down tiling battens which he'd previously treated with preservative. These had been reclaimed when the house was being re-roofed.

Then he came to the laying of slates, a true craftsman's job but one which Albert felt he could tackle. Two new nail holes were drilled into each one using a masonry drill. Once ready, the end slates were cut to size using an abrasive disc on an electric drill.

After the last fiasco with this tool Albert had decided to bear safety in mind. He had searched out some goggles from his collection, and also wore a dust mask. Starting his roofing from the gutter edge Albert ended up with his last row of slates lying below the edge of the conservatory floor. At that point he used a self-adhesive aluminium flashing along the edge of the floor and over the last row of slates. Then another strip of flashing was placed at the floor level and over the edge to overlay the other flashing. It was an excellent job done by someone who had never tackled slate laying before. Nan was especially admiring of Albert's work and was fast becoming one of his adoring fans.

The gardening activity and garage building came to a natural pause at the same time. Without a working compost and incinerator I felt handicapped. Even my repeated desire to 'get a compost going' went unheeded. I knew I'd have to wait until Albert was ready to deal with that aspect of the blueprint. His sights were set on the scree slope and its renovation.

Summer had arrived and with it came my display of annuals. Nemesia, marigolds, and cosmos backed by tall pink, red and blue lupins were a joy to look at. Tomatoes in the greenhouse were beginning to flush. Potatoes in the vegetable bed had already flowered and I was waiting for them to die down before harvesting our first batch of 'earlies'. Albert's rallying call was answered without too much reluctance. I was happy with the results in my garden.

Back into my overalls I laboured once again, helping to clear the offending slope of several tons of rubble, broken glass and sundry items of rubbish.

It was whilst we were working on earth removal and clearance of rock ledges that we came across the broken sewage pipes which led down from the house. They ran in a hand-hewn channel through the rock. Because of their location, work to replace them was precarious and difficult. That put a hold on our step building project.

The unscheduled halt gave me another period of free time. I filled it by clearing more rubble from the lower flower beds at the foot of the slope. On the blueprint a rose arch had been sketched in to span a proposed shingle path between the beds. That walkway would run from the steps to the greenhouse where it would widen and turn, stepping down to the lawn.

The arch of rough tree posts was waiting in Albert's workshop. He had made it one rainy morning during an enforced work stoppage. It only needed completion of the `Steps of Life' for it to be set in place. In anticipation I had purchased a special climber. Night Light was growing on in a pot behind the greenhouse.

When the steps and path were finished I intended to plant it up so that it would flower the following June. Its unusual waxy yellow flowers, which turned to red over a period of two weeks or more, were a sight to behold once it was established. Each subsequent year their delicate perfume filled the garden.

Once the pipes had been replaced Albert returned to the problem of laying steps. It wasn't a straightforward job as we wanted them to follow the nooks and crannies of the quarry face. Sections of rock on different levels were to be converted later into the proposed hanging gardens.

It was a slow and tedious job as he could only prepare two or three steps at a time. These had to be left to harden before the shuttering could be removed and re-set ready for laying the next group of steps.

Of course, Basil had to get in on the act by leaving his paw print in wet cement, as if he was a star of Hollywood's Chinese Theatre. Had I known then what a problem he would become I wouldn't have used Fish, Bone and Blood to start off my first plants. He was to dig up those new beds several times before I realised what the attraction was.

Eventually, the flight of steps was finished. They curved delightfully around the base of the over-hanging rock face, reaching up to the unpaved area outside the back door.

As he'd worked Albert had noted several obvious places which could be mini-terraced into rock gardens. With the steps in place he was able to start work on building up retaining walls, using a variety of natural ledges to take the footings.

Within a week of the steps and hanging gardens being made ready I'd planted a sedum spectabile in the top bed. A Mrs. Popple fuchsia was established in the middle and larger bed, whilst several varieties of aubreitas were planted in the lowest and shallowest hanging garden. This sat above a 3 foot vertical slab of rock which backed another area marked out for terracing on the blueprint. Eventually I intended to have three more beds which would incorporate the all-important 'Fossil'.

Several years later I was rewarded by the original plantings of aubreita re-seeding themselves in rock crevices which criss-crossed the hanging gardens. The quarry face, cleared of ivy, became inhabited by masses of self-sown wallflowers. Yellow and bronze blooms filled the air with a subtle perfume each Spring.

The whole effect was spectacular. All the effort had produced remarkable results which brought a wonderful sense of achievement.

To complete the picture I eventually added dark blue campanula and yellow canary creeper, both of which gradually drifted down the rock face. Amongst them I planted white osteospermum, and a flowering un-identified succulent which had originated in Crete. Covered with miniature deep pink rosettes, its evergreen glossy foliage spread rapidly. Rampant growth within a couple of years meant that it had to be cut back each Spring, before it could take over the steps and conservatory.

That was to be our next major project, the `Pavilion of Enjoying Gardens in the Rain'. In the meantime I continued to gather all burnable refuse and pile it in the corner of the garden hoping that the sight of this growing mound might nudge Albert to start work on the incinerator.

It was marked on the blueprint, but only in pencil, it's importance not yet recognised by the civil engineer. As a frustrated gatherer of rubbish I knew how valuable it would be if I could only get Albert to make a move.

# CHAPTER TEN

Work became bogged down by dreadful autumn weather. The sun vanished behind cloud which rolled in relentlessly from the south west. For days we peered through rain-lashed windows wondering when we'd be able to return to the blueprints which lay idle on the work bench.

We had hoped to make a start on the conservatory before winter set in. I had already set cuttings of geraniums, fuchsias and osteospermums and was badly in need of extra space, the greenhouse being full of tender plants rescued from the garden.

Albert had drafted plans and we'd located a local carpenter who had given us an excellent quotation to do the basic work. The idea was that once the joinery was complete then Albert would do all the detailed finishing off prior to the glazier being brought in. Panelling inside and out, plastering the stone wall where the conservatory butted onto the house and adding carved, ornamental coving were all within his ambit.

Frustration, brought on by inclement weather, helped to focus Albert's mind.
'If I can't get on with the conservatory then I might as well make a start on the work area.'

At last the birth of my incinerator and compost appeared imminent. With each dry period between showers he moved onto site with spade and pickaxe. Gradually the area was levelled and marked out.

It lay out of sight between the summerhouse and the quarry face. My planned lonicera nitida hedge alongside the veg garden-cum-future-pond would eventually enclose and camouflage both the work area and the cave where the scaffolding was stored. There would be a double compost so that I could use one whilst working the other. The incinerator would be built alongside, nearer to the corner of the garden so that a storage for logs could be set alongside.

Albert's idea was that it would be a true work area. Any dead trees could be sawn up and stored next to the incinerator, where they would be dried ready for use in the house during the winter. Already we'd noted several diseased elms overhanging the quarry face. Eventually they would have to be felled.

The new twin composter was to be built out of limestone bricks left over from our original order. Albert's design was well planned. It would be an open lattice work structure which would allow movement of air through the rotting vegetation. Shaped like the letter E lying on its side, the compost bins would sit adjacent to each other but their openings would face away from the summerhouse and towards the incinerator. That was for ease of transferring ash from fire to bin.

Finally, roofing would be made by overlapping strips of flooring left over from inside the house. Banded together they would make three large slats to cover both composts.

The first half of the construction work went well. It turned out to be far easier than anticipated. With several fine days Albert was able to complete the bins and move on quickly to building the incinerator. That was quite a different story.

Also built of pale grey brick this solid three-sided structure would be finished with a large slab of concrete. Albert had already worked out the measurements, set out precise formwork and poured the concrete. All that was needed was completion of the firebox itself.

When everything was in place then a large piece of drainpipe would be cemented into a pre-set hole in the concrete. It was intended to act as a chimney stack. That, in turn, would be topped with a piece of wire mesh to prevent flying sparks from getting into the surrounding forest trees. The idea looked fine on paper. Only the actual method of putting it into practice remained untested.

All construction was completed to Albert's satisfation. Within seven days, spread over nearly three weeks due to interruptions by weather, he was ready to set the concrete slab in place.

On reaching that final stage we realised that an error had been made in the original assessment. It was too large and heavy for one person to move. Without a moments hesitation I was seconded. It needed the strength of both of us to lift it up to shoulder height and drop it onto the walls.

Had we still been in our youth it would have been easily done. As it was the passing years had taken their toll. We were faced with an horrific problem but were determined to beat it. A couple of hours after beginning the back-breaking task we had managed to get it balanced across one corner. We stood back, hearts pounding, and surveyed the next move. Deciding that we had yet another problem we adjourned for a necessary stimulant, the proverbial cup of tea.

How to shift the heavy slab into place across the three walls? That was the question. Neither of us had the energy to lift it further onto the walls of the firebox, yet somehow it had to be moved.

Finally, Albert scrambled inside and slowly inched the slab into its resting place using his shoulder as a lever. Of course, I was cruel enough to want to capture it on film, making him

At last the compost bins and incinerator are finished. D-Day sees Albert lighting his inaugural fire.

kneel beneath the concrete, his head protruding through a tiny gap. That was a humorous shot for the memory book.

Glad to have finished, we left Albert's handiwork for several days, giving the whole structure time to dry out and settle before lighting our first fire.

That day dawned bright and sunny. There wasn't a cloud in the sky. Birds were warbling in the forest trees and the incinerator was piled high with the jetsum which I had collected. Placed on a grating inside the firebox was a mass of ivy mixed with rotting branches of elder, ash, elm and sycamore. Bundles of dried weeds, pulled from behind the caravan, had been added at the last minute. I was determined to make Albert's first fire a good one.

As he carefully laid newspapers and slivers of wood in the space beneath the grill I hovered around with my camera. It was to be an historic moment worthy of note. With lens focused I watched as he lit his rolled paper taper and held it beneath the pyre.

'Whoosh....' It went up like a bonfire as soon as he touched the tinder. Forced back by the sudden heat he quickly vanished behind a cloud of smoke which curled and danced wildly as it billowed from the front opening. A thick grey black column rose from the chimney. As it swirled overhead, fingers dissipating amongst the overhanging branches, I thought I heard the birds begin to cough.

Our incinerator was well and truly alight, but not as had been intended. Sparks and suffocating smoke came from every orifice. We could do nothing but laugh and wait for our first burning to fizzle out.

Back at the drawing-board Albert worked on a solution. He decided to produce a metal blower, using the lathe in his workshop, so that once the fire was lit he'd be able to partially cover the front. That way the fire would draw properly and smoke would be redirected up the chimney, as was intended originally.

Another trial run and the idea proved to be a success. So we were ready to down tools for the winter and take a well-earned break from the heavy work. Albert, of course, vanished into his basement whilst I took to working in my darkroom.

'I need to find more storage space.' His words didn't surprise me when we discussed the day's plans one December morning.
'Thought I'd lower the ceiling by adding a half floor in the main workshop.' I knew that he'd been toying with the idea of altering the basement for sometime.

Once thought out on paper he moved on with the construction, using materials from his squirrel hoard. Metal scaffolding poles were set up against the outside wall. To match, on the opposite wall, was an already constructed stone ledge which protruded 3 feet into the basement. Like a chimney breast, yet without any sign of a fireplace, it was a mystery. Nevertheless, it came in useful as a base on which to lay the ends of cross beams which stretched from the scaffolding.

Not wanting to have further expense Albert unearthed more interior doors which he used as flooring for his new storage space. The only thing missing was some means of reaching the area which was at least 8 feet above the floor.

Finally, Albert decided that the easiest method would be to have a ladder nearby which could be brought out when necessary. As a consquence, he set about hammering hooks and metal rods into the stone wall which divided the main part of his basement.

Eventually that wall was taken over by a kaleidoscope of items, both used and unused. His racing bicycle hung from the ceiling, whilst ladders, old motorcycle helmets, and other sundry goodies found their way onto the display wall. It looked like a small boy's treasure trove, as indeed it was.

In the other half of the basement he had been squirreling away several more motorcycles. His intention was to start work on them when the house renovations were complete.

That part of the property had become Albert's private inner sanctum not long after the builders had moved out. Rarely was I invited in, but on the occasions when I was I'd noticed that he'd made it rather cosy. An old car seat was hidden away in one corner, a nook where he did most of his motorcycle thinking. Nearby was an ancient electric fire, whilst his radio sat to one side of his workbench.

That most important area was set in front of the window where it could receive most light. The only thing missing was the kettle and teapot, or even a keg of beer. Of course, neither were necessary as he had the caravan on hand and it was always ready for visitors.

All his tools were arrayed neatly on the wall close to his lathe, whilst boxes and tins of nuts, bolts, screws, valves, cables and other sundries were stored on numbered and labelled shelves in a side room.

At the far side of the motorcycle collection Albert had built a short staircase leading up to another secret storage area. The ceiling up there was little above head height, and already he'd assembled shelving to take a collection of used and defunct pistons, cans of oil and a variety of engine parts. It was also intended to be the dark area in which to store my wine, when I got round to brewing.

Altogether, the basement was an intriguing place open only to those who had a specific invitation to visit. I was near the top of the list.

Winter arrived, bringing high winds, rain and snow. Of necessity we moved inside, putting erection of the conservatory back on hold.

I planted up trays of seeds which sprouted happily in the dining-room. Fortunately we didn't expect any visitors so I was able to set up several miniature propagators using re-cycled plastic containers which had once contained supermarket produce. These took up most of the dining table leaving barely enough room for us to sit and eat. We agreed to be relocated at one end. The important thing was having plants, and more plants to fill the garden the following year. Having them in the dining room at the early stage of their growth meant that I could keep an eye on them through the cold months of the year.

On the other hand, Albert couldn't complain as he often used my cooker to heat up engine parts, usually when I was away from home. He reckoned that if he lived on his own the house would be full of pistons, valves and complete motorcycles. As a couple, preoccupied with their own interests which often interlaced, we were a well matched pair.

Christmas came and went. We spent it contentedly on our own. Our several children and grandchildren, who lived in far flung corners of the world, kept in touch via letter and telephone.

Quickly we moved into January always keeping busy with plans for the house, garden and travelling. By the time February arrived the weather had begun to pick up so we contacted the joiner.

'Yes,' he'd agreed, 'if the weather stays like this I should be able to get the conservatory up in good time.' So we agreed that he should start straight away.

As we had hoped, everything went along smoothly. The framework went up quickly and Albert was ready to do the finishing off. He began by dealing with the gaps left between the rafters and the house wall. Carefully he filled them with timber fillets and covered the area with aluminium flashing. I was impressed by his knowledge of house building by this time.

Other gaps, between the upright timbers and the house wall, were quite large due to irregularities in the stone wall itself. This needed some ingenious treatment. Albert cut some waterproof plywood to shape with a jigsaw and nailed it into place. Then he moved on to work on the outside.

Because he had decided to use shiplap boarding around the base he had to nail moulding onto the lower cross straps. That gave him a base for the shiplap sections which overlapped horizontally. Before attaching them he lined the frame with heavy duty plastic sheeting to form a waterproof backing. The finished building looked tidy and professional.

At last the glaziers were brought in and heavy sheets of wired cast glass were installed in the roof sections. Windows of clear float glass completed the project and we had our conservatory.

Final small but important details caused the most trouble, especially when it came to sealing all roof spars with self-adhesive flashing. Albert had to erect his scaffolding in order to reach across the wide roof panels. When he came to attaching the ornamental spar along the main beam he had to resort to a tricky manoeuvre. At that stage of the work he opted to run a long ladder out of the bathroom window running it horizontally across the roof to the scaffolding at the garden end. It appeared perilous from my viewpoint on top of the quarry face. Out came the camera. I had to capture Albert crawling across the ladder, hammer in hand and determined look on his face. I was sure that in later years Albert wouldn't believe the risks he had taken to achieve our 5 year goal.

With another stage completed we were ready to move on to building of the deck, but I was beginning to get itchy feet. With the weather closing in yet again I suggested that we take a break.
'Where to?'
'Let's try Madeira.' I slipped the travel brochure into Albert's hand. 'It's known as the Island of Flowers so it should give me some new ideas.'

We both grinned because travelling was another important part of our lives. One which we were always ready to down tools for.

## CHAPTER ELEVEN

We returned refreshed and bursting with ideas to improve on our basic plans.

To begin with, the original deck was planned as a platform from the lounge door. It was designed to be an easy way to get to the conservatory without going through the house, out of the back door and down the steps.

This unusual arrangement had come about because of the difficulty of adding a conservatory directly to the lounge on the second floor. So it was erected on top of the garage and used as an extra room, our 'Pavilion of Enjoying Gardens in the Rain.'

When we returned from Madeira Albert had revised the platform's design. It would now be a large area which would take several chairs, table and garden umbrella.
 'I'll cantilever it from the wall, and keep the steps as originally planned.'

He sounded confident. So confident that I knew he wouldn't need me. It was fortunate that another tempting travel offer had dropped through our letterbox whilst we'd been away. At the same time I was having withdrawal symptoms. I hadn't been able to capture the fascination of the Orient for a long time.
 'Would you mind if I flew off to China for ten days?'
I felt a little tentative, wondering how he would feel about it.
 'No problem. If you'd asked me to go with you I'd have declined. No way would I want to eat with chopsticks for all that time.'

Albert's Morgan runs out of steam. Basil, our ever-willing Jack Russell, lends a paw – on the end of a washing-line.

So plans were made. When I finally left on my adventure Albert was busy building the steps. Already he'd planned the stages of his attack and ten days later I returned to find the deck in place.

'But, what about the steps?' I asked, as I admired the rest of his project.

'Well, that's where I ran into difficulties. I built them in the basement but forgot that I had to lift them up to the deck. So, here they are, waiting for me to think of a way to raise them. They're too heavy to carry round the long way.'

As he described how he'd dealt with the building work I listened with fascination. It seems that he'd first bolted a heavy beam along the house wall just below the lounge doorway. The scaffolding had come in useful once again as he'd had to have somewhere to balance the end of cross beams which would take the floor.

To hold the whole 10 foot square deck in place he'd ordered a couple of specially made flanged metal columns. These were bolted to the deck beams and left hanging until he'd got the deck level. Then they'd been concreted into the ground outside his basement.

Finally, he'd finished it off with a wooden balustrade which had been stained to a warm brown colour. The whole construction was a credit to his ingenuity. It was no mean feat for a man in his 60's working singlehanded. Now his main problem was the staircase. But it was soon solved.

As an engineer he knew how a block and tackle worked, so he built one. As I watched from the garden he carefully hoisted the heavy staircase up to the conservatory where the outside decking was wide enough to take it. Then slowly he lifted it the last few yards, leaving its feet on the garage roof, outside one of the conservatory's doors, whilst the top end was bolted to metal straps beneath the deck.

From across the `crazy' lawn, in front of the still growing leylandii hedge, we were able to look at Albert's remarkable achievement. The rear elevation of the cottage-cum-house had been transformed. Even Unneighbour must have heard about it because one day, shortly after it was finished, we caught sight of him snatching a glance as he drove past on the back lane. How I wished I could have read his thoughts. Especially as the leylandii were then well over the rear wall.

The years were passing. Our 5 year plan D-day was within sight yet we still had a lot to do. There was the patio outside Albert's basement, the `potting shed', the side path and secret garden, the front path, drive and shrubbery, the top garden and finally the wildlife pond.

With every step forward we seemed to move backwards. Always something unforeseen sidetracked us. Not only that, but Albert was fretting for his metal mistresses. Whenever the weather improved he itched to get a bike out and go for a ride in the hills of Snowdonia.

We came to an agreement. We would try and balance the 5 year plan with fairly good stretches of time for leisure activities. Travelling, motorcycling, photography, writing, all would have to be allocated some space in our extremely busy lives.

So it was with renewed energy that Albert set about tackling the side path which had long been a problem whenever the rains came. He decided that it should be concreted in such a way that it wouldn't get slippery when wet. That meant ridging the concrete as it was laid. Once again he built his shuttering, completing alternate sections up the steep incline. The whole project was finished in record time so he was able to move on to the next project, the rebuilding of steps and potting shed.

The Garden Beyond the Window presents a colourful view to those who enjoy the peace of living in the Pavilion for Visitors.

He began with the 'loo' where massive spiders had made their homes. First he attacked the roof which wasn't a roof at all. It was a rusting corrugated sheet covered with turf. That would be replaced with slates once the rest of the area was altered.

Next he took on a grassed slope which ran down to the steps from my temporary strawberry bed. It needed a new stone retaining wall before he could get rid of the weeds and grass. It was an ideal place for another hanging garden, breaking up the height of the wall.

Now he'd reached the main section of sloping grass. To level it he dug it all up, sieving the soil as he went and moving it into the bed behind the new wall.

My turn had arrived. Under direction I moved the strawberry plants into grow-bags outside the greenhouse where they could enjoy full sun for most of the summer. Then Albert built up the stone wall which had held back the soil, leaving me to add more home-made compost to bring the level up to match the height of the new wall.

It was a difficult bed to work because of its situation, lying between the steep path and more steps on the house side. Not only that, it was now at waist height which meant that I had difficulty reaching the back of the bed. As a consequence I changed my planting blueprint, opting to have iris and dwarf hypericum intermixed with a variety of bulbs.

Once I'd worked the soil thoroughly I planted Nan's fuchsia, a dark purple and cream beauty, alongside a Mrs. Popple. They were meant to drape themselves over the high wall in company with another small ivy, the pretty gold leaf. It was set so that it could cascade down to the new strip of grass.

The wall near the shed left me with a sheltered niche, just right to bed in a passion flower. As Albert had added a drainpipe and new guttering, at the same time as the slate roof, I persuaded him to turn the downspout into that enclosed bed thus making sure that the soil never really dried out. My hope was that the passion flower would climb up to the top garden.

When all work had eventually finished I planted up the hanging garden with a yellow alyssum saxatile and bright red coral bells heuchera, both cuttings from elsewhere in the garden. Each spring I scattered nasturtium seeds which spread and cascaded colourfully down the wall.

Above the hanging garden, where the wall met the new lawn, Albert had constructed a fence of field wire. It was ideal to take a broad leafed ivy, the hedera canariensis. I thought that its dark green leaves, with cream edging, would blend well with the passion flower once it reached up to the fence.

That secret area became a favourite. Surrounded by masses of perfumed lilac it was totally enclosed and private. The house wall, where I'd planted a virginia creeper, was on one side whilst the flowering fence hid it from the back garden. Albert even rescued a discarded wooden seat from the local skip. He cleaned it up, added a coat of varnish and an old cushion from inside the 'van, and hey presto, we had a comfortable hideaway.

Once established it became known as my 'Garden for re-visiting Peru'. Each year I planted seedlings of a favourite annual, the sweet scented Heliotrope. Along with the nasturtiums, which began to reseed themselves, these flowers of South America brought back memories of our exciting adventures in that third world country.

When we paused for breath we found that we were moving on faster than anticipated. Summer was still with us so Albert made a start on his patio. He was anxious to be able to bring

The back garden reaches maturity leaving time to enjoy the Platform for Viewing and the Pavilion for Enjoying the Garden.

From the Platform for Viewing we can look down on the Fossil Garden, the Garden for Talking to the Frogs, and the cave.

his bikes out of the basement and work on them as he basked in the warmth of that unusually pleasant summer.

Whilst I'd been digging out the numerous new beds I'd started to wheelbarrow all rubble to where the patio would be. Consequently, when Albert was ready to level it out, and brick the floor, there was little filling left to do. What extra rubble we needed we took from the bed alongside the garage wall, and another larger bed which I had dug out next to the proposed patio.

Again, the area was sketched out on the blueprint. The brickwork would be laid in a formal pattern. Along its garden edge would be a low dutch wall to take rock plants. Where the patio ran down to the lawn, in front of the caravan, its lines of brickwork would widen leaving plenty of room for Albert to ride his bikes out of the basement.

I also found that there was room for me to site a large stone planter which I potted up with spring bulbs, geraniums, osteospermums and pansies.

In the bed alongside the garage I planted Jackmanii, Ville de Leon and Orientalis clematis. At the corner was another stem cutting of the Masquerade rose which grew freely along the wall. At their feet was a Goldflame spirea which was a picture when its deep pink flowers massed over pale yellowy green leaves.

Over the years I added a cutting of Nan's fuchsia, a dicentra `bleeding heart' (which needed topping up with peat from time to time), and hollyhocks. These last cottage garden flowers rewarded me year after year by growing 10 feet or more up to and through the open steps from the deck.

The opposite bed was originally home to an unknown evergreen tree which umbrellaed like a huge pompom at the corner of the house. Its leaves reminded me of an orange tree yet its clusters of miniature white flowers defeated identification. I left it central to the new bed and surrounded it with peonies, globe thistles, orange lilies, michaelmas daisies and phlox paniculata. Against the house wall I planted a white Montana clematis which eventually became home to a thriving population of wrens. Brought up to the music of Classic FM, humming through the stone wall from our lounge, one cheeky nestling took to sitting on the rail of the deck and singing like Pavarotti.

To the front of the bed I established the roots of a rampant summer flowering Jasmine. It too was adopted by our resident blackbirds which found that its thick sweet smelling foliage made an ideal nesting place in mid-summer. Over the years it gained in height, reaching the deck and having to be diverted along another line so as to make a dappled wall of leaves to the side of the patio.

To finish off that area I set out several hardwood window boxes along the base of the caravan. Sheltered from most inclement weather I managed to grow osteospermums, geraniums and sweet williams year upon year.

These added to the general camouflage of the caravan nestled in its surrounding garden of flowers. A winter jasmine combined with a summer flowering variety and the red roses of Masquerade. A newly added pale pink mallow was carefully tied up against the caravan to create a fountain of flowers over the pebbled pathway.

Completion of the patio meant that we had come to the end of most major work. The back garden needed only to mature leaving us free to move to the long forgotten front garden.

The front garden takes on its summer mantle. Johnson's Blue pelargoniums skirt the feet of sweet smelling roses.

Lavatera grow happily amongst the rocks which border the Garden for Listening to the Birds.

# CHAPTER TWELVE

Since moving in we had deliberately left the front garden to fend for itself except for tidying up once the builders had gone. Weeding at that time was kept to a minimum knowing that major work was planned for later in our 5 year plan.

Once we reached that particular stage I soon discovered that it was filled with some wonderful old plants which had established themselves over the years. These were too good to discard and needed to be incorporated into the overall gardening blueprint.

Clumped at one end, beneath the road wall, were rich blood red peonies partnering deep purple and yellow irises. All were prize specimens. In Spring the rest of that long bed came alive with vivid blue grape hyacinths and nodding heads of acid yellow turks cap lilies. Gradually they would disappear beneath a mass of bluebells and Johnson's Blue geraniums which swamped most of the garden.

Mature lilacs in shades of lavender, purple and white, filled one corner yet I found room to add a pretty yellow laburnum. That was a nostalgic reminder of my own childhood garden where mother had cherished a more mature specimen.

At the head of the steep path was a wild rose which gave a brilliant display of glossy red hips in the autumn. It was intertwined with an old-fashioned honeysuckle which perfumed the garden on warm summer evenings.

The garden itself seemed to stretch disinterestedly across the front of the house. Strip beds lay along each side of an oblong of grass finishing where they met the crumbling path from the front gate.

When we had first arrived it had seemed like a jungle of weeds, overgrown plants and foreign jetsum tossed over the wall from the road. Yet even then we had ideas of how to bring it back to life.

After our first exploration of the property, and purchase of the extra lot, Albert had decided to take a pickaxe to the decrepit path and replace it with another raised bed. He planned to incorporate a curved brick wall which would sweep round from the front border to the original raised bed.

As the intended new drive was at road level it lay much higher than the actual garden. That meant making some drastic changes to existing walls. As an instance, the rotten front gate would have to go, the resulting gap being built up to match the rest of the front wall. It too would eventually have to be rebuilt.

Double gates would have to be purchased and set in place but not before a new boundary wall on that side had been built. The blueprint showed the birth of a shrubbery at the foot of the drive. It would stretch past the back door to the quarry face. There Albert planned a small flight of steps up to the top wooded area, scheduled for rejuvenation far down the list.

The original side boundary wall would be demolished and rebuilt so as to edge the drive. I suggested that it become a dutch wall where I could grow rockery plants.

At the house end a wide gap would be left so that Albert could introduce a shallow flight of steps leading down to the path and front door. There the old concrete would be replaced with rough red bricks set down in a traditional pattern.

With the new shrubbery in mind I had already set cuttings of hebes, lonicera nitida, spiraea, and fuchsias. They were potted

Spring flowers surround the Fossil Garden. The Fossil Fish stands proud beyond the timber arch which leads to the Steps of Life.

The fossil rests on the rock face skirted by red sedum spectabile.

up behind the greenhouse. Offers of a mature snowberry and sumac had been accepted. They too were in large pots waiting to be transplanted.

As ever, Albert quickly got to work beginning first with the shrubbery and boundary wall. That brought a flurry of concerned visitors over ensuing weeks.

`You can't build that wall there,' the stranger's voice was loud and assertive. Its owner was a young man who lived over the road.
`It's our property. You can't build a wall on it.'
`Sorry,' Albert donned his diplomatic hat, `but I think you'll find that we've purchased this piece off the rightful owner.'
`But I'm one of the owners. All six of us (he pointed to the row of terraces where the Dowager lived) own it. That's our septic tank over there.' He pointed authoritatively at the concrete coffin set back towards the road.
`Yes, I know about the tank,' Albert spoke quietly, `but I think you'll find that this piece now belongs to us.' With that he turned back to his wall building. I heard the resigned sigh. The young man didn't. He was too busy grumbling as he marched back across the road.

Of course, Albert was in the right. He knew that when we'd bought the land it had been legally severed from the piece which was not co-owned, but co-used for their joint sewarage sytem.

We heard no more about it until several years later when a new owner made the same mistake. That was soon nipped in the bud.

Our next visitor to make comment was Nan.
`What are you doing there?' she asked one day as Bert pickaxed his way through the rock and rubble where the shrubbery would eventually go.

'Anne's going to plant shrubs. She wants them to shield the side door from those cold easterlies which we seem to get up here.'

'I see. Shouldn't think anything would grow there though. It used to be the local rubbish tip.'

That had already been made evident by the number of old carpets which had been unearthed. Albert had even come across more rotting mattresses and bedsteads.

'We noticed,' he confirmed, ' but Anne seems to think that if she can get her cuttings established they'll take off. She's already got several mature plants ready to go in, so we'll just have to wait and see.'

As it happened, they did grow but Nan wasn't around to admire the variety of flowering evergreens which took root in a bed of rock, old carpet and rubble. They make a wonderful arch over the side path, and help to take the chill off my unheated darkroom.

That particular year had started well, but went downhill rapidly. Nan became ill and died within weeks. Then I started being sick for no particlar reason. Time after time I went down with what seemed like food poisoning but eventually, around Christmas, I was diagnosed as having bowel cancer again. That put a stop to all our plans. Within days I was operated on and a few weeks later started on a 9 month course of chemotherapy. I became a 'high-risk' patient.

Never was I more thankful for the conservatory and deck. Imprisoned by the aftermath of my op I spent many days in the warmth of the 'Pavilion for Enjoying the Gardens in the Rain'. Recovery was slow. Without mobility I resorted to reading and toying with jottings which I had collected over several years of travel to exotic places. From my observation gallery I watched for signs of life in the gardens which had become so important to me.

Chemotherapy has taken its toll. All Anne can do is relax and enjoy the flowers in her Garden for Listening to the Birds.

I rejoiced as the first snowdrops opened their eyes, soon to be followed by miniature daffodils and tulips which had been planted in the hanging gardens. They were closely followed by pockets of orange, red and yellow wallflowers which dotted the quarry face. Soon the `Steps of Life' were a mass of purple and blue aubrieta which continued to flower through an unexpected snow flurry.

When Spring arrived in earnest, and a strengthening sun warmed the air, I moved up to the deck, `The Platform for Viewing the Garden of Memories'. That was when my canvas began to take on the meaning which I had intended for it. Unable to travel, or even to garden for any length of time, I dreamed of distant places with each new flowering in the gardens below. Thus each stroke on my floral painting brought a valuable memory to life and I drew strength from it.

As the days lengthened Albert suggested that he start work on the top garden, above the quarry face.
`You should be able to do a bit up there, and I'll install a bench seat so that you'll be able to sit down when you want to.'

I was happy to go along with him, letting him do all the hard work which at one time would have been my job. I watched as he cleared tons of rubble, old bottles, more bedsteads and mattresses. I watched as he felled the dying elms which had threatened collapse from their perch at the edge of the quarry. I gasped as he scaled ladders held in place by lengths of rope. I held my breath as he sawed through huge branches high in the leafless canopies of overgrown forest trees. I closed my eyes at each loud crack as wood snapped to break away and dangle lazily at the end of a taut rope.

It was like having a grandstand view of a theatrical show. Day after day he worked on alone, felling, sawing, and swinging huge timbers down from a great height.

Week after week saw me struggling to get my strength back. I gardened as much as I could, planting more cuttings and seedlings in the new beds along the edge of the quarry face.

That summer was one of wonder for me. I was still alive. The flowers were more brilliant than I'd seen them before. Every new bud brought a sigh of contentment, yet I didn't appear to be getting any better. Eventually, in November, I decided that I'd had enough. I stopped the chemotherapy treatment and lay back exhausted. I couldn't even walk more than two paces, let alone climb the `Steps of Life'.

I felt that I had reached the end of the road. All I wanted to do was to have Christmas at home with Albert. All thoughts of Unneighbour were washed from my mind. It all seemed like a bad dream. Only memories of family, friends, our adventures and the wonderful people we had met, warmed those darkening days. Our 5 year plan was nearly complete, the goal in sight. With that I had to be content.

Another year dawned. I greeted it with surprise and quiet disbelief. By rights I should have died, like all the others who had been on chemotherapy with me, yet I was still around. With each day I felt strength returning. The dark days of agonizing treatment were behind me and I began to plan for the future.

Due to near total destruction of my digestive system I couldn't eat vegetables any more so I decided it was time to convert the veg garden into that long awaited wildlife pond.

Albert began work straight away. It was another pickaxe job. Depth was an essential part of being able to have fish swimming and playing in the pond. As before, Albert drew up plans. He wanted a bean shaped area, shallow at one end with a pebble ramp for the visiting wildlife. A miniature patio was sketched in, along with a garden bench, set between the lonicera hedge and a reed bed donated by a photographic friend.

He worked hard turning those plans into reality and finally, as he put away his tools, we set off on yet another new adventure. Zimbabwe and Victoria Falls beckoned. It was a test for me, one which filled me with renewed courage. Life looked brighter with each day. I knew that I was going to be able to celebrate the culmination of all those years of hard work set out in our 5 year plan.

# CHAPTER THIRTEEN

At last we are able to sit back and enjoy what we call `our masterpiece, our paradise'.

It has taken far longer than anticipated. The highs and lows, the heartache and jubilation have brought us practically to our destination. Yet, as all artists, gardeners and hobby enthusiasts will know, that last stretch has many diversions.

The house is finished to our satisfaction but the garden is ever changing. Each year brings unexpected deaths along with surprising births. Our resident field mice have a lot to do with the re-design, as have the hedgehog, birds and visiting badgers. Nevertheless, we are content.

Albert's collection has grown, each mechanical child having been brought back to life and ridden around our country lanes. With puffs of blue smoke, throat pricking blasts of fume-filled air, thunderous roars of ancient engines, he has kept the spirit of his youth alive.

His white hair, flattened by the constant use of a crash helmet, tells of an age so far removed from how he really feels. Life for him is meant to be lived. With jubilation he sweeps round corners, sails down hills and drinks in the freedom of a life lived in the saddle. How many other 70 year olds must envy him.

As for me, from a vantage point on the deck, now decorated with a raised solar fountain in the heart of massed potted geraniums, I can look out over a canvas detailed with memories.

The `Garden for seeing the Fossil', coloured throughout the year with rockery plants recalls exciting times spent in Egypt. Cruising on the Nile from Luxor to Aswan. Sailing by felucca to the Island of Sehel, beyond the First Cataract. Exploring the secret, empty shores of Lake Nasser, the Nubian Sea, in search of ancient relics.

The `Steps of Life' never fail to stir memories of China, and one particular visit to the Great Wall, at Bad-a-ling. It was late March. Snow outlined the surrounding hills edged with remains of the Wall which snaked into the distance. Crisp snow even lodged in the shadows at the foot of the main Wall where it towered above the village noisy with market traders from Outer Mongolia.

Taking the route known as the `difficult' one I struggled to keep upright on the ever-steepening path made treacherous by melting ice. Dragging myself up the incline, using a freezing hand-rail anchored into the stone, I was halted mid-way by the arrival of a couple of my young companions.
  `We're going right to the top,' they yelled, their pace uninterrupted in their race to the furthest look-out post.

I remember, it was Easter Sunday in Britain. To mark the day each held a small chocolate egg which they waved in my direction.
  `We're going to eat them when we get there,' they called back as they scrambled up a near vertical stairway which curved out of sight above me. Their voices were muted by the surrounding peaks but the excitement shone from reddened faces.
  `We'll be able to say we ate our Eggs, on Easter Sunday, on the Great Wall of China.'

Their voices faded into the distance but the note of triumph was not lost on either me, or the rest of China who were pushing on up the Wall. Rugged faces, lined and sallow beneath thick brushes of slicked black hair, were quickly transformed by huge grins displaying rows of whiter-than-white teeth. Excitement of the moment was infectious. Like me, that couple had set themselves a goal. Mine was the easiest to achieve yet both were appreciated by our oriental companions who clapped enthusiastically.

China is brought easily to mind through a wide variety of plants dotted around the garden. Senecios and buddleias, chyrsanthemums and sedums all transport us to Shanghai, and our good friend and escort Xu Jian. With impeccable manners, and excellent English, she helped us to discover that unusual city before we moved on to the Bonsai gardens of Suzhou and a cruise on the Grand Canal.

Our `Garden for Listening to the Birds', on top of the quarry face, not only mirrors that second visit, but also another journey to an equally fascinating part of the world, India and Kashmir.

There we had our first elephant ride, saw our first vultures close at hand, admired the Taj Mahal and lived on a houseboat on Dal Lake. We met people, of another colour and faith, who befriended us `the infidels' so far from home. Those memories will always be warm and colourful. The people we met, the accidents we had, the satisfaction we felt at achieving another goal, all serve to colour the canvas which is our garden.

The hedge near the incinerator has been topiaried into a huge caterpillar to remind us of Africa. It shields the lively pond area, a haven for the visiting heron, squirrel, badgers and birds. No, we don't have elephants or crocodiles, only miniature amphibians. It is my own particular `Garden for talking with the Frogs', a romantic dreamer's pastime. Nevertheless, memories of that larger continent still return with a crispness each time Albert and I sit together on the small bench seat alongside the `Frog Patio'.

'D'you remember when we went on that crocodile walk along the banks of the Zambezi?'

Albert always falls for that particular introduction.

'U'hum. I can still see the steam rising off the elephant dung. They were like huge cannon balls, weren't they?'

'S'right. And d'you remember what that game warden said when he found you with your nose practically in it?'

'You mean about how elephants are myopic? Good job we didn't test out his advice about stepping to one side if we saw one coming our way. Never could quite believe that its eyesight is too poor to see you. I bet it would have been able to smell us.'

'Too right. I've never been so frightened in all my life. Pity about the missed photograph though.' That was the 'one that got away' tale. I can still see its huge ears waving like sails in a gale. It was so scary that my finger froze on the camera button.

The secret garden, now screened beyond the caravan by the rampant passion flower and large leafed ivy, is our corner of Peru. The heavy scent of heliotrope conjures up visions of Annie and Kevin through a mist of colourful memories. A bright young couple they had a zest for living which put wings on the feet of the rest of us, a small ageing group.

Our garden has become that paradise which we had planned. Each corner has a story fluttering amongst its foliage. Every flower has the memory of a person embedded in it. My canvas is complete, the picture alive for as long as I need it.

As for my cancer, I've been diagnosed as clear for over 6 years. Maybe I'll have time to add more detail to my canvas which once was a quarry.

The 5 year plan is complete. The house and garden grow on in harmony towards maturity.